# AUGUSTINE ON PRAYER

# AUGUSTINE ON PRAYER

THOMAS A. HAND, O.S.A.

New Edition

CATHOLIC BOOK PUBLISHING CO.
New York

NIHIL OBSTAT: James T. O'Connor, S.T.D.
*Censor Librorum*

IMPRIMATUR: ✠ Joseph T. O'Keefe, D.D.
*Vicar General, Archdiocese of New York*

SPIRITUALITY FOR TODAY SERIES

*A new series designed to make available spiritual books of lasting value*

Volume V

GENERAL EDITOR
John E. Rotelle, O.S.A.

Vol. I: *Give What You Command*
Vol. II: *Christians in the World*
Vol. III: *Council Digest*
Vol. IV: *Saint Augustine*

This book was first published in 1963.

(T-171)

*Dedicated to*
*Our Holy Mother*
*Saint Monica*
*whose valiant Spirit of Prayer*
*contributed so much to*
*the Holy Father*
*Saint Augustine*

# PREFACE

IN each decade of history, new issues surge into the consciousness of the people. Each subject is discussed, written about, and passed onto the next decade, during which it may either fade out of public consciousness or continue to generate interest and debate. Books, too, seem to follow this pattern. A book which serves a given generation will either continue to be read by successive generations or be relegated to the library shelf, having served only for a brief period.

The writings of Saint Augustine have survived not just decades but centuries. There has been no decade since the fifth century during which these writings were not popular and in demand. It may even be safe to say that in almost every theological work from the fifth century onward, there is either a quote from Augustine or a reference to his thought.

Augustine was a man who "was grasped by Jesus Christ" (Philippians 3:12). After his conversion, the importance of prayer became more and more evident to him. He prayed constantly and the richness of his prayers flowed into his writings. He incorporated prayers into his writings as he paused to give God praise and thanks for walking with him on the journey.

This book, *Augustine on Prayer,* is a compilation of the thoughts, words, and prayers of Saint Augustine. It has served former generations as they searched for God and embarked on their own restless journeys. But this book will be valuable to other generations, too, and that is why efforts have been made to reprint it.

When a book is reprinted, a certain amount of adjustment is usually necessary to adapt it for the use of the modern generation. However, very little needed to be done to update this ever-current book. Only some archaic language—principally the use of the words "thee" and "thou"—was changed.

In the reprinting of any book, the author is naturally remembered with fondness and gratitude. As I prepared *Augustine on Prayer* for publication, time and again I thought of the author of the book, Father Thomas Hand, O.S.A., of the

Province of Ireland, Order of Saint Augustine. I never knew Father Hand personally, but I recall how this very book, when first read, nourished my own prayer life and increased my knowledge of Saint Augustine. I am thankful to God for him and for the talents that God gave him.

Father Hand now rests in eternity, but he is still remembered in time by all of us who use this book to prepare ourselves for the journey beyond.

Thank you, Father Hand; we remember you at prayer and at the altar of the Lord. And we give thanks to Almighty God, the source of the talents and the gifts which he allowed you to share with us and generations to follow.

25 March 1986
Annunciation of the Lord
Our Lady of Grace
(Augustinian Calendar)

John E. Rotelle, O.S.A.

# CONTENTS

# INTRODUCTION

Since his death in 430 A.D., writers of every generation have exhausted all the superlatives in paying tribute to the genius of Saint Augustine. But while many of them have tried to tell us in their own words what he taught on almost every subject, they have frequently left us without an adequate idea of what he himself actually said on any subject. Now, if ever there was a man capable of speaking for himself, that man was Augustine. Yet, he is seldom given the opportunity of doing so at any length. In this work, therefore, I have made Augustine speak for himself on the very practical and devotional subject of prayer.

It has never been any part of my intention to produce an academic work. Indeed, it would be very difficult to do so in view of the fact that, for the most part, the material is that of Augustine the pastor of souls preaching to the lay people of his day. It is, therefore, a spiritual book which, nevertheless, has sufficient reference matter appended to make it of interest even to an academic reader. Sincere thanks are due to the Very Reverend James Canon Hamell, D.D., of Saint Patrick's College, Maynooth, and to the Very Reverend Father Aegidius Doolan, O.P., for their patient reading of more than one typescript, for their careful criticism, and for the many genuinely helpful suggestions they so kindly offered.

At the close of his *Rule* Saint Augustine gave the following counsel to those who acknowledge him as their Father in the Religious Life:

> "When you find that you are observing the things that are written here, give thanks to God, the author of every good gift. But if anyone finds himself wanting in some point of observance, let him be sorry for the past, watchful in the future, praying that God may forgive him his trespasses and lead him not into temptation. Amen" (*Rule,* XII, 2).

Strange as it may seem, he never wrote what could be called a treatise on prayer, though he did speak of it in many of his works, in his letters, and of course in his sermons to the people.

During the past few years I have culled more than five hundred texts relevant to prayer from the writings of Augustine, and have endeavored to fit them into his own doctrinal background of happiness, eternal life, grace, love of God, and humanity. Whether this be the manner in which the holy bishop himself would have handled the material, I do not know. But I have made him speak for himself and, consequently, feel justified in calling the work *Saint Augustine on Prayer.*

If there be one thing more than another that may strike the reader — apart from the amazing fullness of Augustine's treatment of the subject in the fifth century — it could well be the necessity of grace for prayer; the fact that prayer is not something we give to ourselves, but is itself a grace or a gift from God. Of special interest also is the unexpected emphasis that Augustine brings to bear on certain aspects of the subject, as for instance in his insistence on the quality of forgiveness in the one who would effectively pray. I have tried to keep any commentary of my own as unobtrusive as possible, so that the full beauty and vigor of Augustine's teaching may come as untouched to the reader as it came to his hearers over fifteen centuries ago; and I quite sincerely make my own the sentiments expressed by him in the last lines of his monumental *City of God:* "May those who think I have said too little, or those who think I have said just enough join me in giving thanks to God. Amen" (XXII, 30).

Thomas A. Hand, O.S.A.

*Saint Augustine's Priory*
*Washington Street*
*Cork*
*2 December 1962*

CHAPTER 1

# PRAYER IN MAN'S QUEST FOR HAPPINESS

## Desire for a Happy Life

"EVERY MAN, whatsoever his condition, desires to be happy," declares Augustine. "There is no man who does not desire this, and each one desires it with such earnestness that he prefers it to all other things; whoever, in fact, desires other things, desires them for this end alone."[1] There are various ways of living adopted by men, "yet, in whatever kind of life he chooses, there is no man who does not wish to be happy."[2] "To aim at the happy life, to wish for the happy life, to covet the happy life, to seek it and follow after it, is, I think, the business of all men."[3] This desire, then, is common to all men; to all men, absolutely — be they good or evil. "He who is good is therefore good that he may be happy; and he who is evil would not be so, if he despaired of the possibility of being happy by that means."[4] But, while no one escapes this universal thirst for happiness, or disputes its existence, nevertheless a good deal of controversy appears to revolve around its object. All men seek happiness: "But to know where to find this thing desired of all; that is disputed among them, that divides them."[5]

Some people seek happiness in wealth;[6] others seek it in honors;[7] others again in the pleasures of the body.[8] More prudent people seek their happiness in knowledge,[9] or in virtue,[10] or, like the philosophers, in wisdom.[11] All of them tend toward the same goal by a multiplicity of ways, and the goal they seek is the delight they hope to enjoy in being happy. And though the ways they follow in search of this enjoyment may differ, still they come to the experience of it by a rhythmic movement of the soul, simple in character and common to all. The first movement is of the intellectual order: they must know the object that offers them happiness. "For who can love what he does not know?"[12] This knowledge, manifestly, must concern the beauty, charm, and attractiveness of the beloved object. Could it possibly engage their attention and animate their hearts without that?[13] The second act is of the sentimental or emotional order. Arrayed in all the attractions that their intelligence discovers in it, the object excites their affections and enkindles an ardent desire in their hearts to possess it.[14] The third act is an act of the will. Having been enticed to yield to the attraction which enthralls it, the will stirs itself, and, translating desire into action, takes possession of the beloved object. That is the moment of delight.[15] It is obvious, however, that while all the faculties cooperate in procuring the beatifying object, the decisive act appertains to the will. And this movement of the will is released by the impulse of an interior power called love. It is this that draws every lover to seek happiness in his beloved.

According to Greek physics all bodies, the smallest as well as the greatest, are carried by their natural weight toward a particular place in the universe. "Fire tends to rise, a stone tends to fall. Drawn by their weight they reach their proper places. Oil released under water makes its way above it. Water poured over oil slides beneath it. Both are carried by their weight toward the place that is proper to them.[16] And this place toward which they are drawn is the place in which they come to rest."[17] Under the impulse of a power given by nature, every body tends toward that state which is natural to it, and in which alone it finds rest and stability. Now, the human soul, according to Augustine, is subject to this same law. "It only tends toward what it loves, so that attaining it, it may find rest."[18] And the power that draws it is like an interior weight that puts pressure on the will, and this power is called love. "Just as the body gravitates according to its weight, so also the soul, in whatever direction its movement tends, is carried along by love."[19]

Love, therefore, is a vital necessity for man; he loves, in fact, as naturally as he breathes. "Not to love is to be cold, to be callous";[20] it is to place oneself beneath inanimate bodies, which respond at least to the traction of their weight. For the human soul also must find its proper place if it would enjoy a happy rest, and in so doing it is carried along by love. But, unlike a stone, which moves with the inexorable necessity of nature's law, the movement of the soul is free.[21] People delight only in what they love, but they love only what they want to love. They permit themselves to be drawn only by what gives them pleasure, but they remain free not to follow it.[22] Love is so far from being inevitable, that its most exquisite pleasure is to choose according to its taste and liking the object of its delight.[23] Quite naturally it will choose the object in which it expects to find the greatest happiness. "For as men find special delight in this thing or that, so have they placed in it their idea of a happy life."[24]

And what an amazing variety and diversity of ideas there are, regarding what gives men happiness! How numerous are the loves of the human soul! More numerous than the hairs of our heads.[25] It is necessary, then, to choose with great care and discernment the love that will most ennoble our lives, and give us the greatest happiness. For it does not follow that everyone who attains what he loves is therefore happy. It all depends on what he loves. "Do we say to you: Love nothing?" demands Augustine. "God forbid! Dull, dead, hateful, miserable shall you be if you love nothing. Love, but take care what you love."[26] It is urgently necessary, therefore, that we know which love, out of the many loves that affect our hearts, will procure for us a truly happy life.

## What Happiness Entails

In common with all other men Augustine also went in quest of a happy life. But he did not seek it like most other men. He was one of the greatest geniuses of all time; a man who felt with exceptional intensity, and expressed with an amazing acuteness and clarity the great needs of the human spirit. He could never rest content with a little happiness now and then, like splashes of color against the drab background of daily drudgery. Fleeting pleasures could never satisfy his questing soul. What he wanted was an ecstasy, and a permanent ecstasy, of life, love, and happiness. The happiness he visualized and sought after was a permanent state of well-being, so perfect as to leave no conceivable desire of his heart unfulfilled. He had observed that a man is not happy if he has not gotten what he desires. What he sought, then, was a perfect form of life in which desire itself finds rest, a state of well-being made perfect by the possession of all accumulated good.[27] What he sought to know was, under what conditions all the desires of the human heart would be stilled, and forever; conditions under which a man might find the full perfection and enjoyment of which his being is capable. Some philosophers held that a man who lived just as he pleased, was a happy man. But what if his pleasure inclined him to evil! Would he still be considered happy? Other philosophers — even though strangers to the worship of God — rejected that opinion; they counted such a man miserable, in proportion to the facility with which his depraved will was translated into action.[28] To be happy, therefore, two things are required: A man must "have all that he wants, and want nothing wrongly."[29] Is that all, then? No. He must not only possess it, he must love it as well.

"In my opinion," says Augustine, "you will not be happy if you are unable to possess what you love, be that what it may; nor can you be happy if you do not love what you have, be it ever so good; nor even if you are able to have what you love, if it be harmful to you. For if you desire what you cannot have, you are tormented; if you acquire what you do not want, you are deceived; if you do not desire what should be acquired, you are not mentally sound. Now, none of these conditions is unaccompanied by a feeling of misery, but misery and happiness cannot abide together in you."[30] To be happy, therefore, a man must have what he loves, and love what he has, and it must be something that will do him no harm. But the question still remains unanswered: What must a man acquire for himself that he may be happy?

Manifestly, it must be an object, the possession and love of which would leave nothing to be desired; an object of such transcendent goodness and beauty, that knowledge, possession, love and enjoyment of it, would leave man in a state of well-being so perfect that nothing could possibly be desired beyond it; an object, moreover, possible of attainment which a man could possess if he so willed; something, furthermore, wholly immune from decay — and from the possibility of loss through disaster — the enjoyment of which would give complete, perfect, everlasting satisfaction. Such an object would be the best and the greatest good imaginable. It would be the Supreme Good. "He, therefore, who inquires how he may attain a happy life, is surely inquiring after nothing else but this: Where is the Supreme Good? In other words, in what does man's Supreme Good reside, not according to the perverse and hasty opinions of men, but according to sure and immovable truth?"[31] For life is happy, "when that which is man's Supreme Good is both loved and possessed."[32] "Not that there are no other goods, but that is called the Supreme Good to which all others are referred. For everyone is happy when he delights in a good for the love of which he desires to have the others, and which he loves, not for the sake of any other, but for its own sake."[33]

Now, this good cannot be something within ourselves; if it were we should never be unhappy. True, the Epicureans identified it with the pleasures of the body, and the Stoics with the virtue of soul. But, the advancing ages of the body from youth to old age, and the fickleness of the soul, commuting as it does between folly and wisdom, virtue and vice, certainly leave much to be desired. On the other hand, neither can we say that the Supreme Good is something inferior to ourselves, for that would place our fulfillment and happiness in something less than our own nature; "and that which gives a happy life, or any part of a happy life, is better than that which receives it."[34] Since, therefore, the Supreme Good is neither in us nor beneath us, it must be above us. "What now remains but God himself in whom resides man's highest good?"[35] Loving and possessing him is what constitutes a happy life. So great a good is happiness that it merits to be called "the gift of God."[36] So great and noble a being is the rational creature, even in its fallen state, that nothing inferior to God suffices to yield it a happy rest — not even itself.[37] "I say, therefore, that he is happy who possesses God."[38]

That God is the Supreme Good is manifest, since good is identified with being. Everything that exists is good insofar as it enjoys some degree of being. "For all existence as such is good."[39] It follows that absolute and perfect good, the Supreme Good, can reside only where there is Infinite Being — Immutable and Everlasting Being. This can be none other than God: "For there is no life that is not of God: God is supreme life and the font of life."[40] Our happiness consists, therefore, in the permanent possession and everlasting love of this Supreme Being, this Supreme Good, which is God. "From all this it will readily occur to anyone that the happiness which an intelligent being desires as its legitimate object is the result of a combination of two things: namely, that it enjoy the Immutable Good, which is God, without interruption;

and that it know with a certainty that is exempt alike from doubt as from error, that it shall abide in that enjoyment forever."[41]

Now, when Augustine had put aside the books of the Platonists to take up and read the Scriptures — *Tolle! Lege!* — he found that the yearning of the human heart for happiness, and the findings of reason concerning man's Supreme Good, were ratified by divine assurance, and buttressed by the authority of divine command: *You shall love the Lord your God with your whole heart, with your whole soul, and with all your mind* (Matthew 22:37). This is the commandment "which leads to the happy life."[42] It imposes absolute obligation. It has no limits, for the measure of this love is the utmost capacity of mind, heart, and soul.[43] Saint Paul assured him of complete satisfaction in this love, because *we know that God makes all things work together for the good of those who have been called according to his decree* (Romans 8:28). It was Saint Paul again who gave him the assurance of permanence in the possession of his Beloved: *For I am certain that neither death nor life, neither angels nor principalities, neither the present nor the future, nor powers, neither height nor depth nor any other creature, will be able to separate us from the love of God that comes to us in Christ Jesus, our Lord* (Romans 8:38-39). It is God, therefore, "in following after whom we live well, in reaching whom we live both well and happily."[44] "You have made us for yourself, O Lord, and our hearts are restless till they rest in you."[45] Our desire for God is the only road that leads to happiness.

## "We Must Adhere to God by Love, and Reach Out for Him in Prayer"

Man's quest for happiness in this life, therefore, consists in following after God. It is obvious that the full attainment of God, and the full resultant delight that shall forever beatify the soul, is reserved for the future life. If we truly desire happiness then, we are, by that very fact, desiring immortality. It cannot be something identified with this life, for if life ends, happiness ends, and the loss of it even in expectation cannot be conducive to our enjoyment. Here below, then, we can go in quest of it only by following after God, and, as it were, reaching out for him. Consequently, the great law of morality is to attach ourselves to God, to adhere to him, a law which, Augustine reminds us, was formulated by the psalmist long ago: *My soul clings fast to you* (Psalm 63:9). "God is good; so that it can be well with no one who deserts him. And among his creatures the rational creature is so great a good, that no other good save God can make it happy."[46] God, therefore, who is our Supreme Good, must be the final object of all our striving and of all our yearning. "The sum of all our goods, and our perfect good, is God. We must not fall short of this, nor seek anything beyond it; the first is dangerous, the other impossible."[47]

In this life, therefore, our most important and pressing duty is to unite ourselves to God by love. Going in quest of God, striving to adhere to him, reaching out for him, makes us good; attaining him, seeing him, securely possessing him, makes us happy. "Following after God is the desire of happiness; to reach God is happiness itself."[48] "How can anything be man's highest good but that in cleaving to which he is happy? Now this is nothing else but God, to whom we can cleave only by affection, by desire, and by love."[49] This makes us good. "For a man is never in so good a state as when his whole life is a journey toward the unchangeable life, and when his affections are wholly fixed upon it."[50] "A man is what his love makes him."[51] "For this is the power of love, that it transforms the lover into the image of the object loved."[52] Now, the love whereby we adhere to God is called charity, and is defined by Augustine as: "The movement of the soul that carries it to the enjoyment of God for his own sake."[53] This love, moreover, needs a medium of expression, and that need is supplied by prayer, which is *the affectionate reaching out of the mind for God.*[54]

Prayer, then, plays a most important part in man's quest for happiness. For the life of a Christian on this earth is conceived by Augustine as the journey of a pilgrim soul toward everlasting life and everlasting happiness. It involves the descent of a loving, redeeming God, and the ascent of a loving, aspiring soul. The only ultimate happiness open to this pilgrim soul is the loving possession of God in the security of eternal life. In the meantime, the Christian's quest of happiness consists in his endeavor to adhere to God, in his efforts to unite himself to God by love, and in his reaching out for God in prayer. There is a wonderful feeling of motion in this conception of the Christian life — the motion that is inherent in all things that grow. The soul's love for God is defined as "the movement" that carries it to the enjoyment of God. And prayer is "the reaching out" of the mind for God. In this moving, growing experience of Christian life man's only sure road to happiness is in his desire for God and, as we shall see, his heart's desire is his prayer. May we not conclude, therefore, that prayer, as Saint Augustine defines it, is also man's road to happiness?

He tells us that it is "the affectionate reaching out of the mind for God." How like Augustine to introduce that word "affectionate"! He never really succeeded in separating theology from devotion or logic from love. For him, to speak or to speculate about God merged spontaneously and irresistibly into the affectionate reaching out of his mind for God. Prayer is the language of the soul's yearning for God; it is the interpreter of the heart's desire. "The mouth speaks through the medium of words; the heart speaks through the medium of its desires. It is your heart's desire that is your prayer."[55] "It is not words that God wants of you, but your hearts."[56] "It is with the heart that we ask; with the heart we seek; and it is to the voice of the heart that the door is opened."[57] In these texts, of course, the term "heart" is used in the scriptural sense, in which it indicates our whole interior and spiritual life and all its faculties. Consequently, it signifies not only the heart, but the mind as well. True, according to Augustine, it is with the heart that we pray. For God wants to hear the call and the cry of a loving heart. But what is this cry of the heart? Augustine himself answers: *the cry of the heart is a solemn earnestness of thought, which, when given vent to in prayer, expresses the profound yearning of the one who prays.*[58] Prayer is the affectionate reaching out of the mind for God; it involves mind and heart, thought and desire, knowledge and love.

## Prayer Is the Heart's Desire

"The whole life of a good Christian is a holy desire."[59] This desire is the unsatisfied yearning of a pilgrim's heart, and the voice of the pilgrim's heart is the voice of his heart's desire. That voice is the only one that penetrates to the ears of God. "He who prays with desire sings in his heart, even though his tongue be silent. But if he prays without desire he is dumb before God, even though his voice sounds in the ears of men."[60] "I may be wanting in sound," exclaims Augustine, "but never let me be wanting in love!"[61] Prayer is not the reverberation of sound; it is the articulation of love. "As the ears of men are attentive to your lips, so are the ears of God inclined to your heart. How many there are whose lips are silent, but whose love is eloquent. So many are heard though their lips do not move, and many are left unanswered in spite of their noisy clamor. We ought to pray, then, with our affections."[62] It is with the heart, rather than with the lips, that we pray.

Augustine observes that prayer actually has a voice of its own, and quite distinct from the voice of the one who prays. This "voice of prayer" is the heart's desire, which, though not audible to human ears, sounds like a cry in the ears of God, and "is called a cry by reason of the intensity of its reaching for God."[63] The psalmist makes it quite clear that prayer has a voice of its own, when he says: *Yet you heard the sound of my pleading when I cried out to you* (Psalm 31:23). Again, he says: *But God has heard; he has hearkened to the sound of my prayer* (Psalm 66:19). And in yet another psalm we find these words: *I say to the Lord, you are my God; hearken, O Lord, to my voice in supplication* (Psalm 140:7). Commenting on this latter psalm, Augustine says: "It is a simple statement indeed, and easy to understand; yet it is worthwhile considering why he did not say simply, 'Hear my prayer.' But, as if he would express more emphatically the affection of his heart, he said, 'The voice of my prayer.' That is, the life of my prayer, the soul of my prayer; not merely what sounds in my words, but what gives life to my words. For all other lifeless noises can be called sounds, but not words. Words belong to those who have souls — to the living. But how many pray to God, who have neither a proper perception of him, nor right thoughts concerning him? Such people may have the sound of prayer, but the voice of prayer they cannot have, for there is no life in their prayers."[64]

"Who can doubt but that cries raised to the Lord in prayer sound in vain if uttered only with the voice of the body and not with the heart fixed on God? But, if they come from the heart, then, they may escape any other man's notice if the physical voice be silent, but they will not escape the notice of God. Therefore, whether we cry to the Lord with the voice of the body — when occasion demands it — or in silence, we must cry from the heart."[65]

## The Use of Words in Prayer

Now, while there is no doubt but that in prayer the primacy rests with the mind and with the heart, nevertheless it would be very wrong to conclude that Augustine scorns the use of ready-made formulas of prayer. Words have their place in the affectionate reaching out of the mind for God; they have vitally important functions to fulfill, and not merely in concentrating our attention and aiding our memory, but, above all, in stimulating our desire. Concerning this very matter he wrote to the Lady Proba: "At certain hours we recall our minds from other cares and business — in which somehow or other desire itself grows cool — to the business of prayer, admonishing ourselves by the words of our prayer to fix attention upon that which we desire, for fear that what had begun to lose heat might become altogether cold, and be finally extinguished if the flame were not more frequently fanned."[66]

Augustine, however, is most insistent upon this that, when we pray, we do not use words for the same purposes as in ordinary human affairs. Normally, we make use of words to teach, to convey information, or to recall something to somebody's attention. And as Adeodatus observed in *The Teacher,* "It is not proper to believe that we teach God anything, or that we remind him of anything."[67] God knows all things. Hence, the advice of Saint Matthew not to talk too much: *Your Father knows what you need before you ask him* (Matthew 6:8). Referring to these very words, Augustine demands: "What is the good of prayer if our Father knows beforehand what we need? A man can say to his neighbor: 'There is no need to say any more; I know what you want.' If then, you know, O Lord, why should I ask."[68] Surely it is a waste of time and energy to ask, seek, and knock, as though trying to convey information to one who knows already!

Let it be said at once, therefore, that the words we use in prayer are not intended for the instruction of God, but for the construction of our own desires. That is what God wishes to accomplish by means of the formulas of prayer. Not that he has any need of them for himself, but in the sense that he makes use of them to build up our desires for heavenly things. That is why he gave us the Lord's Prayer. "These words employed by our Lord Jesus Christ in his prayer constitute the form for the expression of our desires."[69] By using these words we keep in mind the things we ought to desire; by insistently asking for them we develop and intensify our desire for them. "To obtain our petition we ought to urge our case with God, not by words, but by the ideas we cherish in our minds, and by directing these ideas with pure love and sincere desire. The Lord made use of words to teach us these very ideas that by committing them to memory we might recall them when we pray."[70]

This teaching is admirably summed up in the following dialogue passage from *The Teacher*. Having observed that prayer should be made in the temple of the mind, and that God does not seek to be taught or to be reminded by our speech that he may give us what we desire, Augustine puts this question to Adeodatus: " 'Are you not disturbed by the fact that our great Master, in teaching his disciples to pray, taught them certain words, so that it looks as if he taught them what words to use in prayer?' (Adeodatus) 'No. That does not disturb me. For he did not teach them words merely, he taught them by means of words, so that through these words they could keep themselves in constant remembrance. He taught them realities: what they should pray for, and from whom they should ask, when they prayed in their innermost mind, as we have said.' (Augustine) 'You have correctly understood the point.' "[71]

There is no doubt but that Christ himself ratified vocal prayer when he said, *Ask, and you shall receive;* and again when, in answer to a most formal request of his disciples, he gave them the Lord's Prayer. Augustine, consequently, never scorns the use of words or formulas; he insists that these words were put into our mouths by the Master, in order to foster and stimulate our desire for the gifts that he would love to bestow. "When you pray you need piety, not verbosity. *Your Father knows what you need before you ask him* (Matthew 6:8). Do not speak too much, therefore, he knows what you need . . . But he wished you to pray for this reason, that he might give you desire, and that his gifts might not be lightly esteemed; for it is he himself who insinuates this desire."[72] In a word, "The Lord our God requires us to ask, not that our wish may be made known to him — for to him it cannot be unknown — but that through the medium of prayer, that desire may be developed in us by virtue of which we may receive what he is prepared to bestow."[73]

## Prayer and Happiness

The words we use in prayer, therefore, turn our thoughts and desires toward the things that God would love to bestow — if we would only have them. He would give us himself, and in so doing would make us happy forever more. And in giving himself he would give us the Supreme Good, together with the life of eternity, the health of immortality, truth that never deteriorates into folly; love, goodness, and beauty immutable in their everlasting perfection. Augustine refers to these benefits as "the proper objects of enjoyment." All other things must be used as means to the attaining of them. "Those things which are objects of enjoyment," he says, "make us happy. Those things which are objects of use assist us, and, as it were, support us in our efforts toward happiness, so that we can attain the things that make us happy and rest in them."[74] Augustine warns us, however, that "if we set ourselves to enjoy those things which we ought to use, we are hindered in our course, and sometimes even led away from it, so that, becoming entangled in the love of inferior pleasures, we lag behind in, or even turn completely away from, the pursuit of the real and proper objects of enjoyment."[75] That this may not happen, we affectionately turn our minds and hearts to God in prayer.

"A happy life is to be sought from the Lord our God. Many different people have given many different answers when discussing wherein true happiness resides. But why should we go to many teachers or consider many answers to this question? It has been briefly and truly stated in Holy Scripture: *Happy the people whose God is the Lord* (Psalm 144:15)."[76] "Why, then, are our desires scattered over many things? And why, through fear of not praying as we ought, do we ask what we should pray for, and not rather say with the psalmist: *One thing I ask of the Lord, this I seek: To dwell in the house of the Lord all the days of my life, that I may gaze on the loveliness of the Lord and contemplate his temple* (Psalm 27:4)? . . . In order that we may attain this happy life, he who is himself the true Blessed Life has taught us to pray . . ."[77]

"The only true life is the happy life, and there is no happy life that is not also eternal life."[78] Health also is vital to happiness; and real health shall not be enjoyed until *this mortal shall put on immortality.*[79] "True, perfect and everlasting health, which is neither reduced by earthly infirmities nor repaired by corruptible gratification, but which endures with celestial vigor, is animated with a life eternally incorruptible."[80] Since we cannot enjoy everlasting life or immortality here and now, neither can we be perfectly happy in this life — except through hope. "Many have reached boldly through transitory evils to good things that will last. And these no doubt are happy through hope . . . But he who is happy through hope is not yet happy, for he awaits in patient expectation a happiness he does not yet grasp."[81] Nevertheless, he is steadfast in his hope, and his goodwill brings him closer to it. For "he is the nearer to happiness whose will is good, and is directed to that which when attained will make him happy."[82]

"We are not Christians except on account of a future life. Let no one hope for immediate happiness. Let no one promise himself the happiness of this world because he is a Christian."[83] If a Christian is blessed with temporal prosperity, no doubt, he should give thanks to God for it. But if temporal misfortune befall him, then his faith should help him to conquer the present and look to the future. "There are some," complains Augustine, "who do not realize that because they are Christians they must hope in the life to come. Such people imagine that Christ has forsaken them, and that they are Christians to no purpose, as soon as they are afflicted with temporal misfortune. They do not realize that the reason for their being Christians is that they must conquer the present and hope for the future . . . that what God has promised is neither of this life, nor of this earth; that all trials must be endured, so that we may receive and secure what God has promised in eternity."[84]

Someday faith will give place to vision, and the happiness of hope will be happiness realized in the world to come. Augustine assures us that "everything there will be good, and the Supreme God will be the Supreme Good, and he will be present for those to enjoy who love him. And, what is altogether most blessed, it will be certain to be so forever."[85] Whoever attains this will have attained the ultimate happiness open to man. He will have all that he desires and will be incapable of desiring anything together with it that would be unfitting. He will enjoy a state of well-being so perfect as to leave nothing to be desired — forever more. "For in it is the fountain of life, which we must now thirst for in prayer so long as we live in hope, not yet seeing what we hope for, trusting under the shadow of his wings before whom are all our desires, that we may be abundantly satisfied with the fullness of his house, and made to drink of the river of his pleasures. *For with you is the fountain of life, and in your light we see light* (Psalm 36:8-10), when our desire shall be satisfied with good things, when there shall be nothing beyond to be sought after with groaning, but all things shall be possessed by us with rejoicing."[86]

In desiring and praying for happiness, then, we are by that very fact hoping and praying for immortality; for if we desire a happy life, we desire also that it would last forever. "As, therefore, all men wish to be happy, certainly if they wish truly, they wish also to be immortal: for otherwise they could not be happy . . . In order that a man may live happily he must at least be alive. But if life quits him through death, how can a happy life remain with him?"[87] Happiness demands everlasting security, it demands immortality. Augustine declares, therefore, that "no one wrongly desires immortality if human nature is by God's gift capable of it; and if it is not capable of it, then it is not capable of happiness."[88]

Whether human nature is capable of immortality and should aspire to it is no small question. "But if that faith be present which is in those to whom Jesus has given power to become the sons of God, then, there is no question . . . For that faith promises, not by human reasoning but by divine authority, that the whole man, who certainly consists of body and soul, shall be immortal, and on that account truly happy."[89] Not that the guarantee of immortality alone constitutes happiness, for the fallen angels are also immortal. Yet no one can be completely and perfectly happy unless he be immortal. And Augustine tells us that the Son of God became man, precisely in order to convince men of that which seemed incredible, namely, that they could and would be immortal. "For if he who is by nature the Son of God was made Son of Man through mercy, for the sake of the sons of man . . . how much more credible is it that the sons of men by nature should be made the sons of God by the grace of God, in whom alone and from whom alone the blessed can be made partakers of that immortality? That we might be convinced of this the Son of God was made partaker of our mortality."[90] "What has God promised you, mortal man? That you shall live forever. Do you not believe this? Then, do believe it, do believe it. For he has already done something greater than what he has promised. What has he done? He has died for you. What has he promised? That you shall live with him. It is more incredible that the Immortal should die than that a mortal should live forever."[91]

It is almost incredible; yet it is true. One day we shall be immortal; we shall dwell in the house of the Lord forever and see the delight of the Lord. There is no doubt but that it was for this vision of God face to face that the psalmist prayed when he said: *Of you my heart speaks; you my glance seeks; your presence, O Lord, I seek* (Psalm 27:8). Augustine continues that prayer in his own words: "In this search I will continue perseveringly, not seeking anything that is common, by your countenance, O Lord, that I may love you gratis, for I can find nothing more precious. *Turn not away your face from me,* that I may find what I seek. *Turn not aside in anger from your servant,* lest in seeking you I run toward something else . . . Be my helper." How shall I find it if you will not help me? "*Leave me not, neither despise me, O God my Savior.* Scorn not that a mortal should seek the Eternal . . ."[92] So did Augustine reach for God in prayer. Because, then only shall all the desires of the human heart find rest, when God and man are reunited in love, in the happy security of everlasting life. "In order that we may attain this happy life, he who is himself the true Blessed Life has taught us to pray."[93]

CHAPTER 2

# LOVE AND PRAYER ARE GIFTS FROM GOD

## I Am, I Know, I Love

THOUGH AUGUSTINE preferred Plato to other philosophers, he nevertheless deplored the fact that the god of the Platonists, toward whom man should move, makes no move toward man. Holy Scripture, on the contrary, had revealed to him the ineffable condescension (literally) of God toward man; the fact that man's redemption involved, not only the ascent of man toward God, but the descent of God toward man. He began to realize that man owes everything to God, his very existence, no less than his salvation, being a gift or grace from God. The whole range of existence from birth to everlasting life is interpreted by Augustine in terms of the gifts of God; gifts bestowed, moreover, not because of any compulsive need on God's part, but out of the spontaneous overflowing of his love for man. "The love that God has for us is immutable and incomprehensible. For he did not begin to love us from the time we became reconciled to him through the death of his Son. He loved us before the creation of the world, so that we could become his children with his only begotten Son. He loved us, in fact, before there was question of our existence."[1]

There is no doubt but that the gifts of God, and the love to which they bear witness, never ceased to be the object of profound intellectual wonder for Augustine. We can visualize him soliloquizing, perhaps, after this manner: The first gift of God to me is that I am a living being. It is obvious that this primal gift is gratuitous, as I did not exist previously and was, consequently, incapable of meriting anything. The fact that I am alive is not my merited due; God did not owe it to me. By his free gift, therefore, I exist — I am. It is also by God's gift that I know of my origin as a creature of God, which is something I could not have known with any degree of clarity or certainty unless he had revealed it to me.

By his free gift or grace, then, I know whence I am, and what I am — the fruit of God's creative goodness. Finally, it is due to his gift that the mysteries of my spiritual aspirations are clarified. The tendency of my mind toward truth, of my will toward goodness, the irresistible thirst for happiness that is in me, all are at once explained, and given the assurance of fulfillment, by the God who loves me so. It is in the realization of these aspirations that my perfection and happiness reside. But I can only come to the perfection of my being by adhering to God, and to the realization of happiness by loving my God in return. This he not only commands me but helps me to do. By God's grace, therefore, I am, I know, I love. So do I find in myself the image of the Triune God who created me; the image of the Father who is subsistent Being; of the Son who is Word and Wisdom; of the Holy Spirit who is Love.

## God Sends His Son

Man, however, might well have hesitated to aspire to the loving of God had not a formal command been issued to that effect. But God did far more than issue a divine imperative; he demonstrated his ineffable condescension in sending his Son to be man's way toward union with him. "For no one ever succeeds in raising another to the height on which he himself stands, unless he stoops somewhat to the level on which that other is."[2] Speaking to God in his *Confessions,* Augustine says: "I began to search for strength sufficient for the enjoyment of you. But I could not find it until I embraced that *mediator between God and men, the man Christ Jesus* (1 Timothy 2:5) *who is God over all forever blessed* (Romans 9:5); who came calling to me and saying, *I am the way, and the truth, and the life* (John 14:6) . . ."[3]

Nothing kindles our love for God so much as the realization that we ourselves are already the beloved of God. "There is no stronger motive for the birth or growth of love than when one who does not yet love perceives himself to be loved, or when one who loves already either hopes that he may be loved in return, or has proof that he is so loved."[4] But the whole purpose of the Incarnation of Christ was, according to Augustine, to demonstrate

God's great love for us. Because "we first needed to be assured of God's great love for us, lest through despair we might not dare to lift ourselves up to him."[5] In order to make this love tangible for us, God vested in human form the Person most dear to his heart, his only Son, and he charged him to bear to us with ineffable words and sublime acts his message of love.[6] Let us love him, therefore, since *he has loved us* (1 John 4:10).

What this divine Ambassador has done for us no voice can utter or pen describe. We are the prisoners of evil; he burst our bonds. We had wandered in the darkness of error; he led us back to the way of truth. We were depressed and feverish; he gave us back life and health. We were loaded with debts; he redeemed our credit. Finally, to crown our benefits, he died for us, signing with his blood the charter of our salvation and the covenant of his love. "It is the shining proof of God's love toward us that he sent his only begotten Son to die for us."[7] "He sent to us his Word, his only Son, by whose taking flesh to be born and suffer on our behalf, we might come to know for how much man counts with God."[8] "He who made man from the dust and gave him life has given his only Son to death for this creature of his making. The greatness of his love for us, who can explain, who can even adequately imagine?"[9]

Many generations before the coming of Christ the psalmist had prayed, saying: *Teach me O Lord, your way that I may walk in your truth* (Psalm 86:11). According to Augustine that prayer was answered when the Son of God declared, *I am the way, and the truth, and the life* (John 14:6). "Walk by him, the Man, and you come to God. By him you go; to him you go. Do not look for any other way by which to come to him. If he had not graciously agreed to become the way we should have always gone astray. I do not tell you, therefore, to look for the way. The way itself has come to you: arise and walk!"[10] Christ was the interior Master, but, "he became an exterior teacher also, that he might recall us from exterior to interior things. And taking the form of a servant, he deigned to appear in lowliness to the lowly so that his sublimity might become clear to those rising up to him."[11] "From what perversity shall not he be free, who contemplates, loves, and follows the words and deeds of that Manhood in which the Son of Man offered himself to us as an example of Life?"[12]

## Christ the Teacher and Exemplar of Prayer

This exterior teacher has taught us to pray. Because, as we have seen, it is only by loving God that we can adhere to him, and it is the function of prayer not only to give expression to that love, but to enlarge and expand the heart's desire, until it is capable of containing him. "You hear the Master praying; learn, you, to pray. He prayed for this reason, that he might teach you to pray."[13] "The Lord wants you to pray; in the gospel he exhorts you to pray. *Ask,* he says, *and you will receive. Seek, and you will find. Knock, and it will be opened to you. For the one who asks, receives. The one who seeks, finds. The one who knocks, enters* (Matthew 7:7-9) . . . If you would be good, be like a beggarman before the Lord who urges you in the gospel to ask, to seek, to knock."[14]

Preaching on another occasion Augustine said: "You have heard the Lord Jesus, that heavenly Teacher, that faithful Counselor, exhorting you to ask, and you have heard that he is the one who grants your request. You have heard him in the gospel, urging you to seek him insistently and to knock even with importunity. As in the stories of the Unjust Judge (Luke 18), and the Importunate Friend (Luke 11), the Lord multiplies his exhortations, and by every means he incites you to ask, to seek, to knock, until you have obtained your request."[15] Commenting on the story of the Importunate Friend, who roused a man from his bed at midnight with a request for three loaves of bread — and succeeded because of his persistent knocking —Augustine said: "From this the Lord would have us understand that if one who was asleep could be constrained to give, even in spite of himself, and after having been disturbed by the person who asked him, how much more kindly will he give who never sleeps, but who rouses us from sleep that we may ask him!"[16]

Speaking of the prayer of Christ at the Last Supper, Augustine observes that, "if there were any need that the Lord, the only begotten Son, coeternal with the Father, should pray in and after the manner of a servant, he could have done so in silence. But then, while showing himself in an attitude of prayer to the Father, it pleased him to remember that he was our teacher also. So great a teacher, indeed, that not only the discourses he delivered to his disciples, but the prayer also that he made for them to the Father, are for their edification. And if for the edification of those who were there to hear these things, doubtless it was for our instruction also, who would read about them when they were put in writing."[17]

Christ, however, was not content merely to issue precepts and exhortations; to these he added the example of a divinely prayerful life. But since our Divine Lord is both God and Man, and as it would not be fitting to suggest that he prayed as God, Augustine hastens to explain that it is in his humanity that the Word is said to pray. "If you consider the divinity of our Lord Jesus Christ," he says, "who is it that prays? To whom does he pray? Does God pray? To one equal to himself? What reason has he for praying, the ever-Blessed, ever-Almighty, ever-Immutable, the Eternal and coeternal with the Father?" Considering furthermore what he himself thundered forth on the lips of John: *In the beginning was the Word; the Word was in God's presence, and the Word was God. He was present to God in the beginning. Through him all things came into being, and apart from him nothing came to be. Whatever came to be in him, found life, life for the light of men. The light shines on in darkness, a darkness that did not overcome it* (John 1:1-5). Reading so far we find no prayer, no cause for praying, nor occasion for praying, nor disposition for praying. But since he says a little further on: *The Word became flesh and made his dwelling among us,* you find the Majesty to which you pray and the Humanity that prays for you."[18]

## The Spirit of Love

The Man Christ Jesus realized, however, that no amount of teaching or of example would ever bring about the union of man's soul with God unless yet another gift were bestowed, namely, the gift of the Holy Spirit, the Spirit of Love — God's gift of himself. Augustine illustrates the need of this gift, over and above the instruction and example of Christ, by reminding us of the transformation it effected in the Apostle Peter. Simon Peter had certainly received more than adequate instruction and example; yet, before the coming of the Holy Spirit, he most ingloriously denied his Lord. "But after he had received the gift of the Holy Spirit, he preached him whom he had denied; whom he had been afraid to confess, he now had no fear of openly proclaiming. Already, indeed, he had been sufficiently taught by example to know what should be done, but he was not yet inspired with the power to do what he knew; he had received instructions to stand, but he had not yet received the strength to keep him from falling. But after this was supplied by the Holy Spirit he preached Christ even to the death, whom in his fear of death he had previously denied."[19]

It is quite clear, therefore, that the love which so unites the soul with God, that not even the fear of death can separate them, is *poured out in our hearts through the Holy Spirit who has been given to us* (Romans 5:5). For God is not only an object of love — he *is* love. *God is love,* says Saint John, *and he who abides in love abides in God, and God in him* (1 John 4:16). One might think that these three words, *God is love,* give expression to a metaphor or symbol. But that would be an error, as they express the most vital of realities. We must not say that our charity or love is from God in the sense that we say: *Only in God be at rest, my soul, for from him comes my hope* (Psalm 62:6), or, *You have been my stronghold, my refuge in distress* (Psalm 59:17). It has not been said in Scripture that the Lord is our love in that sense. "But it has been said in this way: *God is love,* in the very same sense as it has been said: *God is Spirit* (John 4:24). And he who does not discern this, must ask understanding from the Lord, not an explanation from us, for we cannot say anything more clearly."[20]

Now, the Holy Trinity, wishing to make us partakers of this gift of God, of this love which *is* God, has charged the Holy Spirit to diffuse it in our hearts. This diffusion makes the charity or love that is God ours. But let us not deceive ourselves; it accommodates itself to our humanity. It is not the substantial and subsistent charity of the Holy Trinity, but a communication of its ardors and of its flame.[21] Uncreated in God, it is created in us.[22] Nevertheless, having regard for all proportions between the Creator and the creature, it retains distinct characteristics of divine charity. It is not merely an image or a reflection; it is a real and a living participation; and it *has been poured out in our hearts through the Holy Spirit who has been given to us* (Romans 5:5).

"Love, therefore, which is of God and is God, is especially the Holy Spirit, by whom the Love of God is shed abroad in our hearts, by which Love the whole Trinity dwells in us. Most rightly, therefore, is the Holy Spirit, although he be God, called also the *Gift of God* (Acts 8:12). And by that gift what else can properly be understood except love, which brings to God, without which any other gift of God whatsoever does not bring to God?"[23] Our love for God, therefore, is God's gift to us.[24] It is, moreover, God's gift of himself. "He whom we have loved has given us himself; he has given us that from which our love derives."[25]

This gift of love, however, is not given to us in the first instance whole and entire. It is like a seed planted in the heart, having within itself the capacity to grow. "I do not seek to know for the moment," says Augustine, "the extent of this charity; whether it be great, little, or medium. I ask only if it exists. If it has been born in the heart it will grow in secret, and in growing will perfect itself until it shall never cease to be."[26] The important thing is, that *charity be the root and foundation of your lives* (Ephesians 3:17), that we be ready and willing to cleanse our hearts of all sinful loves, to clear the ground for this precious seed, so that God may have room to operate, and to make us participators in his life and love. "That you may love God, let him dwell in you and love himself through you; that is, let him stir you, kindle you, rouse you to the love of him."[27] This is a process in the development of which we must cooperate every day of our lives.

When the Holy Spirit has been given to a man, "he inflames him to the love of God and of his neighbor."[28] But while this flame of love sheds its light on all the faculties of the soul, its radiance is exercised particularly on the will. Charity takes up its abode in the will.[29] The divine ardor which emanates from it rectifies the will and directs it toward what is good. The will is so affected that it takes a genuine delight in what is good. This goodness in the will is not "a different thing from that charity which the Scripture so loudly proclaims to have come to us from God."[30] This gift from God braces the human will and impels it toward the object of its desire — toward God. "I call charity," says Augustine, "the movement of the soul toward the enjoyment of God for his own sake."[31]

Now, there is no doubt but that prayer plays a most important role in this movement of the pilgrim soul. Because "he toward whom the Lord deals in sweetness, that is, he in whom he mercifully inspires delight in what is good; or to speak more plainly, he to whom is given by God the love of God, and the love of our neighbor for God's sake; he, indeed, ought to pray insistently that this gift may be so increased in him, that he may not only despise all other delights in comparison with it, but also that he may endure any amount of suffering for its sake."[32] Prayer is the articulation of our love for God; it is the affectionate reaching out of the mind for God. But while the desires of our heart find expression in prayer, our prayers in turn are the breezes that fan the flame of our love. It is prayer that develops our desire, and enlarges our heart until it is capable of containing God's gift of himself. "Ask, seek, insist," exhorts Augustine; "by asking and seeking you grow big enough to receive."[33]

Strong desires unlock the heart so that it expands and becomes capable of receiving divine favors. The voice of prayer is the heart's desire. "Oh, that we were passing our pilgrimage in sighs, and loving not the world but continually pushing onward with pious minds to him who hath called us! Longing is the very bosom of the heart. We will attain if with all our power we give way to our yearning. Such for us is the object of divine Scripture, of the congregating of the people, of the celebration of the sacraments, of holy baptism, of singing God's praise, and of this sermon of mine — that this longing may not only be implanted and germinate, but may also expand to such a measure of capacity, as to be fit to take in *what eye has not seen, nor ear heard, nor has it entered into the heart of man to conceive*."[34]

"His gifts are very great, but we are limited in our capacity to receive. So it is said: *Open wide your hearts! Do not yoke yourselves in a mismatch with unbelievers* (2 Corinthians 6:13-14). We will receive a more abundant share of what is really great, in proportion to the simplicity of our faith, the firmness of our hope and the ardor of our desire."[35] "The very effort involved in prayer calms and purifies the heart and makes it large enough for the reception of the divine gifts that are poured into us spiritually."[36] Prayer, therefore, enlarges the heart until it is capable of containing God's gift of himself and of desiring permanent possession of him in everlasting life. "Give me a lover, he will feel that of which I speak; give me one who longs, who hungers, who is a thirsty pilgrim in this wilderness, sighing for the springs of his eternal homeland; give me such a man, he will know what I mean."[37]

## The Spirit of Prayer

Let us mark well, however, that this gift of love is not to be confused with what are commonly called the gifts of the Holy Spirit. It does not divide itself into parts nor does it branch out into species. The exceptional privileges granted to certain men, like the gift of tongues, the gift of prophecy, the gift of miracles, or the more general favors offered to all, like the gifts of fear, of piety, of knowledge, of fortitude, of counsel, of understanding, of wisdom, all have their own proper nature and their own specific value.[38] They all come from the Holy Spirit, but as things annexed to or derived from the fundamental gift and destined to become its agents or auxiliaries. "The Prophet (Isaiah) and the Apostle (Saint Paul), both one and the other, have made equal use of the word gifts in the plural; the reason being, that by the gift which is the Holy Spirit many other gifts which are proper to them as his members are given in common to all the members of Christ. All have not got all the gifts, but some have certain gifts, others have other gifts, though all have the gift itself, the Holy Spirit, from whom flows into each one the gifts that are proper to him. In fact, having cited many gifts in another place, the Apostle continues, saying, *But it is one and the same Spirit who produces all these gifts, distributing them to each as he wills* (1 Corinthians 12:11)."[39]

Now, among the gifts emanating from the gift of the Holy Spirit, we must number the gift of prayer. It would be fatal for us to imagine, therefore, that man gives it to himself. We sometimes act, of course, as if prayer actually were something of our own which we offer to God. Consequently, the realization that our capacity to pray is a gift of God may shed a completely new light on the subject. In one of his sermons Augustine puts this statement into the mouth of one who thinks that prayer is his own property: "I prayed that he (God) might give to me; but in order that I might pray I believed beforehand. Therefore, I gave myself faith, and God gave me what in my belief I prayed for."[40]

Augustine answered after this manner: "Let this difficulty be solved as it is no small one. I understand you to say this, that you have first given something to God, so that he may give you the rest. You have given him your faith and your prayer. Where, then, is that of which the Apostle speaks: For *who has known the mind of the Lord? Or who has been his counselor? Who has given him anything so as to deserve return?* (Romans 11:34-35) See what kind of person you would be! Have you, then, first given to God and given something he never gave you? Have you found something to give? O beggarman, where did you get it? Have you, then, the means to give anything? *Name something you have that you have not received* (1 Corinthians 4:7). You give to God, then, what is God's. He receives from you what he has given you. Had he not first given to you, your penury had remained very empty indeed."[41]

Writing to Sixtus Romanus, who later became Pope Sixtus III (432-440), Augustine insists that prayer is a gift of God: "Lest we think," he wrote, "that the merit of prayer is antecedent to grace — in which case grace would not be a free gift, but a reward that was due — let it be understood our prayer itself is counted among the gifts of grace. As the teacher of the Gentiles says: *The Spirit too helps us in our weakness, for we do not know how to pray as we ought; but the Spirit himself makes intercession for us with groanings which cannot be expressed in speech* (Romans 8:26). And what does *helps us* mean, except it be that *he makes us ask?* It is a very sure sign of one in need, to ask with groaning; but it would be monstrous for us to think that the Holy Spirit is in need of anything. So, the word *help* is used, because he makes us ask, and inspires us with the sentiment of asking and groaning, according to that passage of the gospel: *You yourselves will not be the speakers; the Spirit of your Father will be speaking in you* (Matthew 10:20)."[42] As prayer is the affectionate reaching out of the mind for God, it is manifest that the Holy Spirit has no need of prayer. When we read, therefore, that *the Spirit himself makes intercession for us,* the meaning is, that the Spirit himself causes us to make intercession.

"Let them observe, therefore, how mistaken they are, who think that our asking, seeking, knocking is of ourselves and not given to us; who say that this is the case because grace is preceded by our merits, that grace follows upon our efforts when we ask and receive, seek and find, and have it opened to us when we knock. They will not understand that this also is a divine gift, that we pray; that is, that we ask and seek and knock."[43] "Therefore, no one has true wisdom or true understanding; no one is truly eminent in counsel and fortitude; no one has a pious knowledge or a knowledgeable piety; no one fears God with a chaste fear, unless he has *a spirit of wisdom and of understanding, a spirit of counsel and of strength, a spirit of knowledge and of fear of the Lord* (Isaiah 11:2-3). And as no one has true power, sincere love, and religious sobriety, except through a *strong, loving and wise* spirit (2 Timothy 1:7), so also, without the Spirit of faith no one will rightly believe, and without the Spirit of prayer no one will profitably pray. Not that there are so many Spirits, *but it is one and the same Spirit who produces all these gifts, distributing them to each as he wills* (1 Corinthians 12:11), because *the wind blows where it will. You hear the sound it makes but you do not know where it comes from, or where it goes. So it is with everyone begotten of the Spirit* (John 3:8)."[44]

## The Role of Faith and Hope

Let us remember that God's gift of himself is given to us in a seedling state, and it is in the light of faith that we become conscious of this seed of divine love deposited within us. How should we be able to cultivate and to defend it, if we did not know of its origin and of its holiness? "For who can love what he does not know? It is possible, of course, for something to be known and not loved; but I ask, whether it be possible for what is not known to be loved? If it cannot, then, no one loves God before he knows him. And what is it to know God if not to conceive and steadfastly perceive him with the mind?"[45] But knowledge of the God who is love waits upon recognition of him. To know him is to acknowledge him by faith. And it is faith in Christ that leads to the knowledge, love, and enjoyment of God. That is why the Son of God became man. "Because, if he came as God he would not be recognized; if he came as God it would be of no use to those who could not see God."[46] "But faith is belief in what you do not see, and the reward of that faith is to see what you believe."[47]

It is clear, therefore, that faith plays a unique role in the growth of the love of God in our hearts, for love depends on knowledge. The more faith increases our knowledge of God, the more it exalts our love toward him.[48] Our minds and hearts have a thirst for the seeing of God, even in this life, and faith, at least in part, tears aside the veils that conceal him from us. It discovers the magnificence of the Trinity, the sublimity of the incarnation, the immensity of the redemption, the splendors of the eucharist, the admirable treasures of grace, and the ineffable ecstasy of eternal happiness. However mysterious these revelations may remain to our understanding, the glimpses we are permitted through the eyes of faith dilate our hearts, and give new enthusiasm to our love.[49] On the road to the infinite, faith precedes understanding and points out the reality to be attained.[50] Under the direction of faith, the intellect puts itself to work, and through its analyses and deductions seeks to understand the contents of this reality.[51] Frequently, understanding succeeds, and each one of its conquests enriches the faith. "In the measure that one seeks such a good in order to find it and finds it in order to seek it, one becomes better. One only seeks it, in fact, in order to find it more sweetly still, and one finds it, only to seek it more eagerly still."[52]

But if faith be vital to our growth in the love of God, it is vital also to prayer. "If faith fails, prayer perishes," preached Augustine. "For who prays for what he does not believe? Faith is the source of prayer"; and in order to show that faith is the source of prayer and that a brook cannot run when its fountainhead is dry, the Apostle says: *But how shall they call on him in whom they have not believed?* (Romans 10:14) Therefore, that you may pray, believe, and pray that faith itself, whereby you pray, may not fail you. Faith pours forth prayer, and prayer poured forth implores the strengthening of faith."[53] "In these two prayers — the Creed and the Lord's Prayer — you have those three graces exemplified: faith believes, hope and love pray. But without faith, hope and love cannot exist. Therefore, we may say that faith also prays."[54]

But faith cannot exist without hope.[55] "If you already have faith which works through love, it is necessary that you should hope in what God has promised; for hope is the companion of faith. As long as you do not see what you believe, hope is necessary for fear you fall into despair because you do not see."[56] The vision that faith procures certainly kindles our love; nevertheless, we still see "through a glass, darkly." This saddens our hearts, and we long to sweep the mist from the mirror to get a clearer view.[57] But hope enters in to console our hearts and to sustain the faith which might lose its buoyancy without it. This is not done by argument because hope does not argue. It leaves deductions and conclusions to the mind and addresses itself to the heart. It knows that the heart aspires to everlasting happiness. It says to the heart: This happiness — you shall have it. You wish to see God, not in a misty mirror, but face to face? You shall see him.[58] You wish to possess him completely, without the fear of ever losing him? You shall have him.[59]

These promises of hope are the promises of God, and they carry with them the certitude of realization. What consolation for the heart, what stimulation for charity, what motive power of desiring for prayer! "How could you desire so much to pray to God, if you did not hope in him?"[60] The realization, based on divine authority, that love will have its recompense, bolsters faith, re-enkindles charity, until love feels but one pressing duty: to increase, to grow bigger, to reach forward to the possession of God. That is why love is never idle, knows neither respite nor repose. "Love cannot be idle," declares Augustine. "Show me — if you can — a love that is idle and doing nothing!"[61] As faith increases knowledge, as hope increases expectation, love moves into action and reaches out for God, its yearning expressed in prayer.

Let us acknowledge, therefore, that faith, hope, and charity, love and prayer — all are the gifts of God; we do not give them to ourselves. So much is prayer the gift of God, that the psalmist equates it with the mercy of God in our regard. If a man loses the capacity to pray, it may mean that, for some reason, the mercy of God has been withdrawn from him. Consequently, Augustine exhorted his people to pray without ceasing so that they might enjoy this assurance of God's mercy. He reminded them how eagerly the psalmist acknowledged his indebtedness to God for the gift of prayer. *Blessed be God,* he exclaimed, *who refused me not my prayer or his kindness* (Psalm 66:20). "As long as we are here on earth, therefore, let us also beg God not to take away our prayer and his mercy from us. In other words, let us beseech him that we may always pray and always receive his mercy."[62]

Prayer is the love of God articulating. But let us never forget this, that love and prayer, both, are the gifts of God.

CHAPTER 3

# WHY WE SHOULD PRAY

## That We May Keep God's Commandments

OUR LOVE FOR GOD is measured, not by how we feel, but by how we live; not by sentimentality and emotion, but by our conduct and behavior. *He who obeys the commandments he has from me is the man who loves me,* declared our divine Lord (John 14:21). And again, *Anyone who loves me will be true to my word* (John 14:23). Our union of love with God, therefore, consists in the fulfilling of his will as expressed in the commandments. "I would that you conform your life and behavior to God's commandments, which we have received as the rule of right living,"[1] wrote Augustine. He tells us, furthermore, that to so conform our lives we must pray for divine assistance. "Let us live well; and that we may live well let us invoke the aid of him who has commanded us to live well."[2] But if we would live well and grow in this union of love with God we must avoid evil and do good. And the good we must do and the evil we must avoid are made clear to us in the commandments of God.

"Now, the Lord himself not only shows us what evil we should avoid and what good we should do — which is all the letter of the law can do — he helps us also *turn from evil and do good* (Psalm 37:27), which is something no one can do without the spirit of grace. If this is wanting, the law comes in only to make us guilty and to destroy us. Is is for this reason that the Apostle says: *The written law kills, but the Spirit gives life* (2 Corinthians 3:6). He, therefore, who uses the law lawfully learns good and evil in it if he does not confide in his own strength, but flies rather to grace by the help of which he may avoid evil and do good."[3]

"It is quite obvious that to know the commandments of God is one thing, to keep them is another. The knowledge of them does not of itself impart the power to keep them. Consequently, God's help does not consist in this only, that we have learned by our knowledge."[4] "Strengthen me that I may be able," prayed Augustine. "Give what you command and command what you will."[5] "It is certain that we keep the commandments if we so will, but because the will is prepared by the Lord, we must ask him for such force of will as suffices to make us act by willing. It is certain that it is we who will when we will, but is it he who makes us will what is good . . . It is certain that it is we who act when we act, but it is he who makes us act by supplying efficacious powers to our will."[6]

"He who wishes to keep God's commandments but is unable to do so already has a good will, but as yet a small and delicate one; he will become able, however, when he shall have acquired a great and robust will . . . And who was it who had begun to give him his love, however small, but he who prepares the human will and perfects by his cooperation what he initiates by his operation? For just as he begins his influence by working in us that we may have the will, so does he complete it by working with us when we have the will."[7] God gives us the realization that his *yoke is sweet* by inspiring our wills to find sweetness in doing good; he strengthens our will in its adherence to his commandments by giving us patience in tribulation; he gives us knowledge by insinuating understanding. It was for these things that the psalmist prayed, saying: *Teach me wisdom and knowledge, for in your commands I trust* (Psalm 119:66).

"God, therefore, teaches sweetness by inspiring delight; he teaches discipline by the moderate use of tribulation; he teaches knowledge by the insinuation of understanding. Since, then, there are some things we learn merely that we may know them, and other things we learn that we must also do them, when God teaches he does so in such a manner that we may know what ought to be known by revealing the truth, and do what ought to be done by inspiring sweetness. Not for nothing are these words addressed to him: *Teach me to do your will* (Psalm 143:10). He said, teach me that I may do and not merely that I may know. For the good deeds we do are the fruits we render to our landlord. The Scripture says: *The Lord himself will give his benefits; our land shall yield its increase* (Psalm 85:13). And what is that land but the human soul of which it is said to him who gives sweetness: *My soul thirsts for you like parched land* (Psalm 143:6) . . . Then teach me sweetness by inspiring charity; teach me discipline by giving patience; teach me knowledge by enlightening my understanding, for I have believed your commandments. I believe that you have commanded these things; you, who are God, who gives a man the means of keeping your commandments."[8]

In his homilies on the psalms Augustine frequently reminds us how fervently the psalmist prayed for the gift of the Holy Spirit that he might keep the divine commandments. *I gasp with open mouth in my yearning for your commands* (Psalm 119:131). "What did he long for but to obey God's commandments? But there was no possibility of the weak doing hard things, of a little one doing great things, so he opened his mouth to confess that he could not do them of himself and he drew in the power to do them. He opened his mouth by asking, seeking, knocking; thirsting he drank in the good Spirit which enabled him to do what he could not do of himself — *the commandment is holy and just and good* (Romans 7:12). For if we being evil know how to give good gifts to our children, how much more shall the heavenly Father give the Holy Spirit to them that ask him (see Luke 11:13). For, it is not those who are led by their own spirit, but *all who are led by the Spirit of God are sons of God* (Romans 8:14). Not that they do nothing, but that they may do something good, they are moved by the good Spirit. For so much the more is every man made a good son insofar as the good Spirit is given him by the Father."[9]

The yoke of God's commandments is sweet and light, but only for those who really love God and who find sweetness in doing his will. To those who have given their hearts to the pleasures attendant upon sin, the commands of God are burdensome. "For no other reason," writes Augustine, "does Holy Scripture insist on the truth that God's commandments are not grievous, except that the soul that finds them grievous may understand that it has not yet received those resources of grace that make the Lord's commandments such as they are commended to us as being, that is, gentle and even pleasant, and that the soul may pray in the deep earnestness of sincerity for the gift of a ready facility in keeping them. For the man who says: *Let my heart be perfect in your statutes* (Psalm 119:80); and the one who says: *Steady my footsteps according to your promise, and let no iniquity rule over me* (Psalm 119:133); the man who says: *Your will be done on earth as it is in heaven* (Matthew 6:10); and, *Subject us not to the trial* (Matthew 6:13); and other prayers of a similar import it would take too long to particularize, he does, in effect, offer up a prayer to keep God's commandments. Neither, on the one hand, would any injunctions be laid on us to keep them if our own will had nothing to do in the matter; nor, on the other hand, would there be any room for prayer if our will were alone sufficient."[10]

"God's commandments, therefore, are commended to us as not grievous, so that he to whom they are grievous may understand that he has not yet received the gift that removes their grievousness, and that he may not think he is really keeping them when he keeps them but finds them burdensome. *For God loves a cheerful giver* (2 Corinthians 9:7). Nevertheless, when a man finds God's commandments burdensome, let him not be broken by despair; let him rather be driven to ask, to seek, and to knock."[11]

## That We May Avoid Sin

We have seen that it is good for us to adhere to God and that we adhere to him by loving him. We have seen, furthermore, that loving God involves the keeping of his commandments. Consequently, we must avoid whatever might violate God's commandments and so interfere with our loving adherence to him; that is, we must avoid sin. "For men are separated from God only by sins."[12] And Augustine tells us that we cannot avoid sin unless we have recourse to prayer. "We guard against sin by prayer. When a man wills what is evil and commits sin, his will has been deceived. He must guard against such deception. If it cannot be resisted there is no sin. If it can be resisted and is not submitted to, there is no sin. Whatever may be the cause of this deception it certainly can be resisted, because there are sins committed. This implies that they could have been resisted and were not. Now, it is for this reason that we pray for help, saying: *Subject us not to the test.* We would not ask for help if we supposed that resistance were impossible. It is possible to guard against sin, but only by the help of him who cannot be deceived."[13]

Man's good, man's virtue, man's happiness, consists in the soul's adherence to God by love. A man must make choice of this because it is the express will of God. He must be subject to God on this vital issue if he would retain his mastery over other inferior creatures that God made for his use and benefit. If a man freely expresses preference for a lesser rather than the Supreme Good, he has been deceived; but that deception involves a capitulation within the soul itself for which man is responsible. This is what constitutes sin. "Therefore, sin is a real inordination and perversion in man, a turning away from the most excellent Creator and a turning toward inferior creatures."[14] "What is evil is the will's aversion from the changeless good and its conversion, being voluntary and not compelled, is followed by the fit and just punishment of misery."[15] Sin, then, consists in a transference of love from the supreme to a lesser good. And since our union with God is our love for God as manifested in the fulfilling of his will, there is no sin that does not separate us from God. Its misery consists in this, that God relinquishes the sinner to his disorderly love, leaving him to be the slave of things that were created beneath him. *God delivered them up in their lusts to unclean practices* (Romans 1:24). *I give you my assurance, everyone who lives in sin is the slave of sin* (John 8:34).

"On all sides is the beauty of the work that commends the Maker to you. You admire the workmanship; then love the Craftsman. Be not too preoccupied with what was made and so withdraw from him who made it. He who made you beneath himself made these things with which you are preoccupied beneath you. If you cling to him who is above you, you will trample under foot what is beneath you; if you withdraw from him who is above you, these things will be turned into misery for you. For this is the case, my brethren; man received a body to serve him, having God as his Lord and his body as his servant; having above him his Creator and below him what was created inferior to him; while the reasonable soul, set in a sort of middle ground, had a law laid upon it to cling to him who is above it so as to control what is below it. It cannot rule what is below it unless it be ruled by him who is above it. If it be seduced by what is beneath it, it has abandoned him who is better than itself."[16] In order that this may be avoided we must persevere in prayer, which is the affectionate reaching out of the mind for God.

About the year 416 Augustine and his good friends Alypius, Evodius, and Possidius wrote a joint letter to His Holiness Pope Innocent concerning the teachings of Pelagius. In that letter they maintained that when a man makes the petition, *Subject us not to the test,* he is, in effect, praying for help that he may avoid sin. "He prays, therefore, not to commit sin, that is, not to do any evil. And that is what the Apostle asks in prayer for the Corinthians, when he says: *We pray God that you may do no evil* (2 Corinthians 13:7). From this it is quite clear that though the freedom of the will is called into play in refraining from sin, that is, in doing no evil, still, its power is not efficacious unless there is help forthcoming for its weakness. Therefore, the Lord's Prayer itself is the clearest testimony of grace. Let Pelagius admit this and we shall rejoice over him as being in the right, or as having been set right."[17]

Augustine observed, furthermore, that the inspired writers in Scripture prayed frequently to be delivered from the enemies of their souls' salvation. The psalmist prayed, *Rescue me from the clutches of my enemies and my persecutors* (Psalm 31:16). "The devil and his angels, these are the enemies against whom we pray. They envy us the kingdom of heaven; they would not have us ascend to the place from which they were cast down. From these let us pray that our souls may be delivered."[18] *Resist the devil and he will take flight,* says Saint James (James 4:7). Even the followers of Pelagius held this. But Augustine remarks: "There is this difference between us and his partisans, that whenever the devil has to be resisted, we not only do not deny, we actually teach, that God's help must be sought for; whereas they attribute so much power to the human will as to take prayer out of our religious duty."[19] "If any man says that we ought not to use the prayer, *Subject us not to the test* — and he says as much who maintains that God's help is not necessary to avoid sin, and that a person's own will after accepting the law is sufficient for that purpose — then, I do not hesitate to affirm at once that such a man ought to be removed from the public ear and have his anathema pronounced by every tongue."[20]

*Who can free me from this body under the power of death?* prayed Saint Paul (Romans 7:24). A man makes this prayer, according to Augustine, because he desires "to be strengthened against sinning in future. For he delights in the law of God after the inner man, but sees another law in his members fighting against the law in his mind (see Romans 7:22-23). Observe this, that he sees there IS such a law; he does not recall it as if it were in the past. It is a present pressure, not a past memory . . . Hence, that cry of his: 'O, wretched man that I am! Who shall deliver me from the body of this death?' Let him pray. Let him beg for help from the mighty Physician. Why gainsay that prayer? Why shout down that entreaty?"[21]

## That We May Not Enter Into Temptation

"Every temptation is a test," declares Augustine, "and every test applied bears its own fruit. For the most part you are unknown even to yourself; you do not really know what you are able or unable to bear. Sometimes you presume to withstand what is beyond you; at other times you despair of being able to cope with what you could well bear. Temptation comes, as it were, in the form of a question, and you are found out by yourself because you did not know even your own self."[22] Now, the temptation that assails us may be one or the other of two kinds. It may be the kind that deceives us; on the other hand, it may be the type that subjects us to a kind of test that reveals our moral strength or our moral weakness. "This latter God makes use of, not to learn something that he himself did not previously know, but that by tempting you, by drawing you out, he may reveal what is hidden in you. For within you lie things hidden even from yourself in whom they reside. These things are discovered, brought out in the open and exposed, only by temptations. If God should cease to permit temptation, the Master would cease to teach."[23] "It is not good for you to be without temptation. Do not, therefore, ask God not to be tempted, but not to be led into temptation."[24]

To enter into temptation, or to be led into it, means to be subjected to a temptation under the pressure of which we shall surely fall. "We are led into them if they are such that we cannot endure."[25] It means being abandoned by God in time of temptation because of our self-reliance. "But God turned away his countenance from the one who said, *I shall never be disturbed* (Psalm 30:7), and that one was confounded and shown to himself."[26] Consequently, we must pray never to be so abandoned by God. We may rest assured that we shall never be completely free from temptation of some kind or other, for the life of man on earth is a temptation. *My son, when you come to serve the Lord, prepare yourself for trials* (Sirach 2:1). "Wherefore, our heavenly Master also says: *Be on guard, and pray that you may not undergo the test* (Matthew 26:41) . . . He does not enter into temptation who conquers his evil desire by the bent of his will to do good. And yet the human will is insufficient to refuse to enter into temptation unless the Lord grant it victory in answer to prayer. What indeed offers clearer evidence of the grace of God than the granting of what is prayed for? If our Savior had said merely: *Be on guard that you may not undergo the test,* he would evidently have done nothing but admonish man's will; but since he added the words, *and pray,* he indicated that God helps us not to be led into it."[27]

The effort of the human will, then, is not enough of itself to conquer temptation. Nevertheless, that effort must be made, and the reinforcing strength of grace should be asked of God in prayer. "No man is assisted by God unless he himself also does something. He is assisted, however, if he prays . . ."[28] Writing on the petitions, *Subject us not to the trial but deliver us from the evil one,* Augustine asks: "Why, indeed, do we present such petitions in earnest supplication if the result is of him that wills, and of him that runs, but not of God that shows mercy? Not that the result is quite independent of our will, but that our will does not accomplish its aims in action unless it receives divine assistance. Now the wholesome effect of faith is this — that it makes us ask that we may receive, seek that we may find, and knock that it may be opened to us. Whereas the man who disputes this, closes the door of God's mercy against himself."[29]

Writing on another occasion against the Pelagians, who exaggerated the power of the human will both in doing good and avoiding evil, Augustine said: "They are beginning to corrupt the minds of their hearers, and it must be said with sorrow that they are hostile to the grace of Christ, for they would persuade us to regard as unnecessary the prayer to the Lord that we enter not into temptation. As champions of the freewill of man they try to prove that we can fulfill the divine commandments by our will alone and without the assistance of God's grace. From this teaching it would follow that the Lord spoke to no purpose when he said, *Be on guard, and pray that you may not undergo the test;* and that we say daily in the Lord's Prayer itself, and to no purpose, *Subject us not to the trial.* If to overcome temptation is already in our power, why do we pray not to enter into it or not to be led into it?"[30]

Finally, in a letter to Pope Anastasius, Augustine again condemns these champions of the unaided human will. "Through their argument," he wrote, "the weakness of men, wretched and needy as it is, is convinced that we ought not to pray lest we enter into temptation. Not that they dare say this openly, but whether they like it or not this conclusion certainly follows from their theory. For what use is there of his saying, *Be on guard, and pray that you may not undergo the test* and what use, when after this exhortation he was teaching us to pray, that he instructed us to say, *Subject us not to the trial,* if this is not to be fulfilled by the help of divine grace, but to rest entirely with the human will? What more is there to say?"[31]

## That We May Advance In Perfection

"As far as perfection is concerned, I can say this to you, briefly: *You shall love the Lord your God with your whole heart, with your whole soul, and with all your mind,* and *You shall love your neighbor as yourself* (Matthew 22:37, 39). These are the words in which our Lord when on earth gave an epitome of religion, saying in the gospel: *On these two commandments the whole law is based, and the prophets as well* (Matthew 22:40). Advance, then, daily in this love both by prayer and good works, that by the help of him who so commanded you, and whose gift it is, it may be nourished and increased until, being perfected in you, it may make you perfect. For this is the love which, as the Apostle says, *has been poured out in our hearts through the Holy Spirit who has been given to us* (Romans 5:5)."[32]

Augustine maintains that, "We must by no means deny to human nature the power of perfectibility since we admit its capacity for progress — by God's grace, however, through Jesus Christ our Lord."[33] "We assert that human nature becomes holy and happy by the assistance of him who created it to be so."[34] "There is no method whereby people arrive at absolute perfection, or whereby any man makes the slightest progress toward true and godly righteousness, but by the assisting grace of our crucified Savior, Christ, and the gift of his Spirit — and whosoever shall deny this cannot rightly, I think, be considered a Christian at all."[35] To advance in perfection we need grace; to grow in grace we must have recourse to prayer. No man gives it to himself; it is the gift of God.

This God-given love for God is the criterion and the measure of our progress. "Great in some souls, less in others, nonexistent in some; there is no one in this life so perfect that he cannot increase in it. But as long as he can increase, that which he lacks of what he ought to be is beyond doubt a defect."[36] Consequently, we must reach forward and strive to advance daily in this love. There is perpetual motion in the spiritual life, the motion that is inherent in growth. "Charity knows nothing but to increase more and more."[37] It is not born in us in a state of perfect development. "It is born that it may be perfected," says Augustine, "and when born it is nourished; when nourished it is strengthened; when strengthened it is made perfect."[38]

The love, therefore, whereby we adhere to God is given to us in a seedling state and it needs a favorable ground in which to grow. To make room for that seed to grow we must clear the ground of our souls of all pernicious growth, that is, of all adherence to the world. This is the labor and the battle of a lifetime. "In this life there are two loves fighting one against the other in every temptation, the love of the world and the love of God, and whichever of these gains the victory draws its lover in its train as by a weight. Christ came to change our love and to transform the lover of earth into a lover of the celestial life. This is the combat proposed to you: to subdue the flesh, to conquer the devil, to wage war on the world. But have confidence. He who declared this war does not look on without offering to help you: nor does he exhort you to rely on your own strength."[39]

"For even this very thing that man can live justly, as far as man can live justly, is not the fruit of human merit, but of divine beneficence."[40] "To live a good life is the gift of God," because by the Holy Spirit he pours forth charity in the heart of man.[41] This indwelling love, which is God's gift of himself, must express itself in action, and by so doing it grows. "All our good works are one work of charity, for love is the fulfilling of the law."[42] So the gift becomes a virtue, and is, according to Augustine, not the only virtue, but the principal virtue, having all other virtues under its command by means of which it attains its end. For even though charity commands all the virtues it is in the practice of these virtues that it conserves and augments itself, or rather, it is by performing acts of virtue as yet imperfect that it elevates itself from an imperfect charity to a charity that is more and more perfect. These virtues, says the holy bishop, "are like the army of a general whose headquarters is within your soul. And just as a general does what he wants through his army, so the Lord Jesus Christ, when he begins to inhabit our inner man, makes use of these virtues as if they were so many instruments of his will."[43]

"Our righteousness in this pilgrimage of absence is such that we press forward to that full and perfect righteousness where love shall be fulfilled and perfected in the vision of his glory. We accomplish this by the rectitude and perfection of our lives, by disciplining our bodies and mastering them (see 1 Corinthians 9:27), by giving alms cheerfully and heartily, by bestowing kindnesses and forgiving trespasses committed against us, and by persevering in prayer (see Romans 12:12). By doing all this, moreover, with sound doctrine whereby a right faith, a firm hope, and a pure charity are constructed. This is our righteousness now in which we pass through our course here, hungering and thirsting after that perfect righteousness that shall delight us hereafter.

Therefore, after our Lord had said in the Gospel, *Be on guard against performing religious acts for people to see* (Matthew 6:1) — that we might not measure our course in life by the limits of human glory — he goes on to expound righteousness itself, but he points out only these three constituents of it: fasting, alms, and prayers. In fasting he indicates the complete subjugation of the body; in alms he indicates all kindness of will and deed either in giving or forgiving; in prayer he indicates all the rules of holy desire . . . *In that case, run so as to win!* (1 Corinthians 9:24)."[44]

To demonstrate the progress of the pilgrim soul Augustine avails himself of the seven gifts of the Holy Spirit (Isaiah 11:2-3), presenting them as stages in the pilgrim's progress toward perfect union with God. And to show the necessity of prayer on this pilgrimage he tells us that the seven petitions of the Lord's Prayer may be interpreted as having reference to the seven gifts of the Holy Spirit.[45] This correspondence of the petitions of the Lord's Prayer with the stages of our spiritual progress is a fundamental trait in the spirituality of Saint Augustine. The steps we take toward union with God are taken in an atmosphere of prayer. They are in point of fact a continual prayer, for prayer is the affectionate reaching out of the mind for God. It is prayer that gives expression to the heart's desire for the perfecting of its love for God. It is prayer, furthermore, that constructs that desire until the heart is capable of embracing God himself.

"Let us not fall back, then, to the point from which we started," exhorts Augustine, "neither let us remain stationary in the spot at which we have arrived. Let us run. Let us reach forward. We are on the way. Do not feel safe because of what you have passed on the way, but anxious rather because of what you have not as yet attained."[46] "Let us run by believing, by hoping, by desiring. Let us run by subjugating the body, by doing kindnesses and forgiving injuries. The strength of the contestants will be helped by prayer. And let us listen to the commandments that urge us on to perfection so as not to neglect running toward the fullness of charity."[47]

## That We May Persevere Unto The End

In conclusion, the Bishop of Hippo reminds us that prayer is necessary for perseverance, which he defines as: "A fixed and lasting constancy in a well-considered resolve."[48] "I make the assertion," he declares, "that the perseverance whereby you continue in Christ unto the end is a great gift of God. The end, however, to which I refer is the end of this life wherein alone lies the danger of your falling. As long as you live, therefore, it is uncertain that you have received this gift; for if you fall away before you die, I say, and I say most truly that you did not persevere."[49] "How much is it to be feared that the ship may be diverted and turned back! This happens when, abandoning the hope of heavenly rewards, desire turns the helm and man directs his gaze with distorted cupidity to the visible and transitory things of earth."[50] We must pray that this may not happen because perseverance is given only on condition that we ask for it. "It is evident that God will give some things, like the beginning of faith, even to those who do not pray, and that he has reserved other things, like perseverance unto the end, exclusively for those who do pray."[51]

"When the Apostle says: *We pray God that you may do no evil* (2 Corinthians 13:7), beyond doubt he prays to God on their behalf for perseverance . . . And in that other place, moreover, where he says: *I give thanks to my God every time I think of you —which is constantly, in every prayer I utter — rejoicing, as I plead on your behalf, at the way you have all continually helped promote the gospel from the very first day. I am sure of this much: that he who has begun the good work in you will carry it through to completion, right up to the day of Christ Jesus* (Philippians 1:3-6) — what else does he promise them from the mercy of God but perseverance in good unto the end? . . . And no one need doubt that whoever prays from the Lord that he may persevere in good, confesses by that very act that such perseverance is a gift from God."[52]

Augustine teaches that the necessity of prayer for perseverance has always been the faith of the Church. "As the Church has been born and grows and has grown in these prayers, so it has been born and grows and has grown in this faith, by which it is believed that God's grace is not given according to the merits of the receivers . . . For the Church would not pray that it might persevere in the faith of Christ, neither deceived nor overcome by the temptations of the world, unless it believed that the Lord has our hearts in his power in such a manner that the good we do not hold save by our own will, would not be held except he worked in us to will also. For if the Church asks these things of him but thinks that they are given by itself, it makes use of prayers which would be not true but perfunctory. May such prayers be far from us! For who truly sighs, desiring to receive what he prays for from the Lord, if he thinks that he receives it from himself and not from God?"[53]

"Fix your gaze on him who leads you and do not look back to the place from which he brought you. He who leads you goes ahead of you; the place from which he brought you lies behind you. Love your leader for fear he may condemn you for looking backward."[54] "Forget the things that lie behind you, forget your past life of sin, and reach forward to those things that are before you."[55] "Let no one look back; let no one delight himself with his former interests; let no one turn from what lies ahead to that which is now behind; let him run until he arrives — and we run, not with our feet, but by the power of our desiring. But never let anyone say that he has reached it in this life."[56]

If it be tiring to advance always and perseveringly in perfection, Augustine directs our attention to the reward in store for us and urges us to imitate the example of those pilgrims who sing as they march along. "The time of faith is a laborious time, who denies it? But this labor has as a recompense an eternity of happiness."[57] It is from this happy fact that he derives the cheerful spirit in which this pilgrimage of ours should be run. Speaking of the paradise in store for us he says: "O, the happy Alleluias there! . . . There is praise given to God; here on earth is praise given to God. But here by those full of anxious care; there by those free from care. Here by those whose lot it is to die; there by those who live forever. Here in hope; there in hope realized. Here on the way; there in our fatherland. Now, then, my brethren, let us sing;

not for pleasure as we rest, but to cheer us in our labor. As pilgrims are wont to sing, sing, and travel on . . . If you are making progress you are marching on; but progress in good, progress in the true faith, progress in right living — sing, and travel on!"[58] This spiritual slogan of Augustine, *Canta et ambula,* has been rendered as "Sing, and travel on," or again as "Sing, and march on," but the real spirit of Augustine's *Canta et ambula* is, "Sing, and soldier on!"

Prayer is necessary on every stage of our journey, that we may avoid evil and do good; that we may not be led into temptation; that we may grow in the love of God and so advance in perfection; finally, that we may persevere unto the end. The soul is a pilgrim homeward bound and prayer is the pilgrim's song. And the theme of the pilgrim's prayer-song is epitomized in this petition of the psalmist: *One thing I ask of the Lord; this I ask: to dwell in the house of the Lord all the days of my life, that I may gaze on the loveliness of the Lord and contemplate his temple* (Psalm 27:4). In order that we may one day enjoy that truly happy life, he who is true life has taught us to pray. And when that prayer is finally answered, our pilgrimage shall have ended, and a happy permanent perfection shall be established when perseverance and salvation shall have been realized. "The end, therefore, of our purpose is Christ, for however much we attempt, in him and by him we are made perfect. And this is our perfection, that we come home to him."[59]

CHAPTER 4

# FOR WHAT AND FOR WHOM WE SHOULD PRAY

## For God Himself

WERE WE TO ASK Augustine what we should pray for, he might well answer and say that "it is lawful to pray for what it is lawful to desire."[1] But since right order must be observed in our desiring, a corresponding order should be manifest in our requesting. "He lives justly and devoutly who appraises things in their entirety. Such a one has a well-ordered love; for he neither loves what is not to be loved, nor fails to love what should be loved, nor loves to excess what should be little loved, nor loves equally what should be more or less loved, nor loves more or less what should be equally loved."[2] But what is the right order of love? "The order in which you can have true love and real charity, the Lord himself has told you and plainly shown you in the Gospel, for he speaks after this manner: *You shall love the Lord your God with your whole heart, with your whole soul, and with all your mind . . . you shall love your neighbor as yourself* (Matthew 22:37, 39)."[3] Our first love, therefore, and the principal object of our prayer should be God himself. "In this life," says Augustine, "virtue is nothing else but the love of that which ought to be loved. To choose this is prudence; not to be turned away from it by any difficulty is fortitude; or by any seducement, and that is temperance; or by any pride, and that is justice. But what must one choose for one's first love if not that Good than which there is no better? That is God. And if we place any other thing over him in our love, or on the same level, we do not know how to love ourselves."[4] To love ourselves properly, therefore, we must have a love of conscious preference for God, and this should find expression in our prayer.

Augustine maintains that our love for ourselves is inborn, and for that reason we never needed a commandment to love ourselves. "In every man the primary object of love is self, and love can have no beginning unless it begins with self. No one has to be advised to love himself."[5] So, even though there are three divinely appointed objects of love, namely, God, ourselves, and our neighbor, nevertheless, only two precepts were given to us. "It was not said, 'on these three,' but *on these two commandments the whole law is based, and the prophets as well* (Matthew 22:40), that is to say, on the love of God with one's whole soul and heart and mind, and on the love of the neighbor as one's self. This was done so as to make it understood that there is no other way of loving one's self save in loving God."[6] "Love God, love your neighbor: God as God, your neighbor as yourself. There is no other equal to God, so that you might be bidden to love God as you love that other. But for your neighbor you are shown a rule, since you yourself are shown as your neighbor's equal . . . May I now entrust to you your neighbor to be loved as yourself? I should like to do so, but I am as yet afraid to do it . . . I still need to probe the nature of your love for yourself."[7]

There is no doubt but that a man can love himself wrongly, that he can love himself to his own detriment. "Some people think that they lawfully love themselves when they seize the goods of others, when they steep themselves in drink, and they pander to their lusts, or when they reap unjust gains by various means of deception. Let such people listen to the words of Scripture: *He who loves iniquity hates his own soul* (Psalm 11:6). If by loving iniquity you not only do not love yourself but even hate yourself, how will you be able to love either God or your neighbor? If, therefore, you would follow the order of true charity, do justice, love mercy, flee sensuality, begin to love according to the precept of the Lord, not only friends, but enemies. And when you have tried faithfully to observe these precepts, you will be able by means of these virtues to ascend, as it were, by steps, until you merit to love God with all your mind and with all your strength."[8] "He, therefore, who knows how to love himself, loves God; but he who does not love God, even if he does love himself — a thing implanted in him by nature — is rightly said to hate himself, inasmuch as he does what is prejudicial to himself and assails himself as if he were his own enemy."[9] "The more we love God, the more we love ourselves."[10]

If, therefore, we would love ourselves wholesomely, we must love God more than ourselves. He must be our first love, and that quality of conscious preference should find expression in prayer, that is, in the affectionate reaching out of our minds for God. "What, then, shall you pray for? Why, surely, what the Lord, your heavenly teacher, has taught you to pray for. Call upon God as God, love God as God. There is nothing preferable to him; desire him, yearn after him. Listen to the psalmist who in another psalm calls upon God and says: *One thing I ask of the Lord; this I seek* (Psalm 27:4). And what is it that he asks of the Lord? *To dwell in the house of the Lord all the days of my life, that I may gaze on the loveliness of the Lord* (Psalm 27:4). If, then, you would really be the Lord's lover, choose him from your inmost heart, yearn for him with holy desire, love him, be all aglow with him, look eagerly for him, because you will find nothing more delightful, nothing that can fill you with more joy, nothing better, nothing more lasting. What could be more lasting than he who is everlasting?"[11]

In Augustine's day people prayed to pagan gods for material goods and for preservation from temporal evils. The god Neptune was supposed to preserve sailors from shipwreck. The goddess Juno, wife of Jupiter, was supposed to guarantee a safe delivery to expectant mothers. Speaking against such pagan beliefs, Augustine said: "Even having regard to this world, by whom is anything given to man but by God? Or what is taken away from man except what he who gave, orders, or permits? But vain men imagine that these demons whom they adore give it. Sometimes they say to themselves that God is necessary for life eternal and for the spiritual life, but that we ought to worship these other powers for the sake of temporal things . . . God, however, will not be worshiped together with them, not even if he be worshiped much more and they much less . . . Of all that worship Neptune, have none suffered shipwreck? Of all that blaspheme Neptune, have none arrived in port? Have all those women who worship Juno had a good delivery? . . . If they ought to be worshiped for the sake of these temporal things, then their worshipers alone would be richly endowed with temporal blessings. And indeed, even if this were so, we ought to avoid such gifts and make one petition of the Lord."[12]

*Aloud to God I cry; aloud to God to hear me* (Psalm 77:2), says the psalmist. Many people call on God in prayer but the voice of their heart's desire is not directed to God. They endeavor to make God the minister of some material gain which is the sole object of their desire and of their prayer. They ask for almost anything but the gift of God himself. "It has been said of some men: *They cried for help — but no one saved them; to the Lord — but he answered them not* (Psalm 18:42). Why? Because their voice was not directed to the Lord. The Scripture expresses this in another place where it says of such men: *They have not called upon the Lord* (Psalm 14:4) . . . They have not called the Lord unto themselves; they have not invited the Lord into their hearts; they would not have themselves inhabited by the Lord. And what happened to them? *Then they shall be in great fear* (Psalm 14:5). They feared the loss of present things because they were not full of him on whom they called."[13] "God fills your heart, not your purse."[14] "If God came to you without gold and silver would you have nothing to do with him? Of all those things that God has made, what is sufficient for you if God does not suffice you? With good reason, then, does the psalmist pray: *O Lord, let me not be put to shame, for I call upon you* (Psalm 31:18). Call upon the Lord, brethren, if you would not be shamed."[15] "To call upon him, or to call him to you, means to invite him, so to speak, into the home of your heart."[16]

The following lament of Augustine is just as apt today as it was fifteen hundred years ago: "Many cry to the Lord to avoid losses or to acquire riches, for the safety of their friends or the security of their homes, for temporal felicity or worldly distinction, yes, even for mere physical health which is the sole inheritance of the poor man. For such things many cry to the Lord, but scarcely one for the sake of the Lord himself. Alas, it is easy to want things from God and not to want God himself, as though the gift could ever be preferable to the giver."[17] We must not conclude from this, however, that the safety of our friends, the security of our homes, and good health are things unworthy of our desire or of our prayers. Nothing could be further from the mind of Augustine. We love everything that God gives (*amor*), but when there is a question of a love of conscious preference (*dilectio*) we love God above all things.

"God does not forbid the love of these things but only the finding of our happiness in the love of them. We should make the love of their Creator the end of our esteem for them. Suppose, brethren, a man should make a ring for his betrothed and she should love the ring more than her betrothed. Would not her heart be convicted of infidelity in respect of the very gift of her betrothed, though what she loved were what he gave? By all means let her love his gift. But if she should say, 'The ring is enough, I do not wish to see him again,' what would we say of her? . . . The pledge is given by the betrothed just so that in his pledge he himself may be loved. God, then, has given you all things: love him who made them."[18]

"The asking is with the heart, the seeking is with the heart, and the opening is to the heart. Now, the heart which asks rightly, which seeks and knocks rightly, must be pious. It must first love God for his own sake, for that is piety, and not propose to itself any reward which it looks for from God other than God himself. For there is nothing better than he. What precious thing can he ask of God by whom God himself is lightly esteemed?"[19] The love of God will find its truest expression in the prayer that is offered for his own sake and not for the sake of anything he may bestow. In a word, we should love God gratis. "Ask nothing from him but the gift of himself."[20] "To hope for God, from God; this it is to love God gratis."[21]

"Leave, then, all other desires. He who made heaven and earth is more beautiful than all things. He who made all is better than all. He who made beautiful things is more beautiful than all . . . He will be for you everything that you love. Learn, then, to love the Creator in the creature, and, in the work, the one who made it. Never permit what was made by him to take such a hold upon you that you lose him by whom you yourself were made."[22] "Whatever comes from God is unjustly loved if he be forsaken because of it."[23] "Ask in this present time for what may help you in eternity, but him love gratis. You will find nothing that he may give better than himself; but if you can find a better thing, by all means ask for it."[24] "He who seeks any other reward from God and is willing to serve him because of it, makes that which he desires more precious than him from whom he desires it. Has God, then, no reward? None — except himself."[25] "Make us happy, O my God, in our concern for you, that we may not lose you."[26]

## For Temporal Things — in Moderation

It is well to remember that while God promises heaven, he does not desert us on earth. "He who cared that the earth should be, does not neglect his image on earth."[27] It would be very wrong for us to conclude, therefore, that Augustine would have us desire and pray exclusively for eternal benefits and ignore the material necessities of life on this earth as if they were evil in themselves. *Everything God created is good* (1 Timothy 4:4), declares Saint Paul, and we may quite lawfully love them, provided God is not abandoned because of them. It is well to remember, also, that Adam did not sin by desiring something evil in itself, but by abandoning something better. "Every tree that God planted in Paradise was good. Man, therefore, did not desire anything evil by nature when he touched the forbidden tree. But by departing from what was better, he himself committed an act that was evil. The Creator is better than any creature, and his command should not have been disobeyed by touching what was forbidden — even though it was good. The better was abandoned and a created good was coveted in contravention of the Creator's command. God had not planted a bad tree in Paradise. But he who had forbidden that tree to be touched was better than the tree."[28]

There are many natural pleasures associated with our mortal state in which we may quite lawfully take pleasure, provided we love righteousness more. We are not expected to shun them as if they were evil in themselves, but we should steadfastly refuse to put them on a higher plane than God or on the same level of importance as moral integrity or moral beauty. Once again it is a question of the right order of love. While we love all things that God made, we preserve a love of conscious preference for their

Creator. All things are good, but they need good men to put them to good use.[29] "A holy psalm sweetly intoned delights the ear, but the songs of stage-players delight the ear also. The one lawfully, the other perhaps unlawfully. Flowers and perfumes delight the sense of smell, and these too are God's creatures, but frankincense on the altars of devils delights the sense of smell also. The one lawfully, the other unlawfully . . . You see, dearly beloved, that in these senses of the body there are lawful and unlawful delights. Let righteousness so delight as to dominate even lawful delight. Yes, prefer righteousness to that pleasure with which you are delighted even lawfully."[30]

But, since it is lawful to pray for what it is lawful to desire, and since temporal goods are lawfully desirable, it is quite in order to pray for them. We may pray, therefore, for health and friendship, for a happy marriage, healthy children, a comfortable home, for sufficient wealth to ensure the upkeep of appearances befitting our state in life. For such things any man may quite lawfully pray, so that, as Augustine says, "he may appear as he ought among his neighbors, retain their respect, and discharge the duties of his state in life."[31] "It is not unbecoming for anyone to desire enough for livelihood and no more: because this sufficiency is required, not for its own sake, but for the good of the body. Nor is it unbecoming that we should desire to be clothed in a manner befitting our station, so as not to be out of keeping with those among whom we have to live . . . Accordingly, we ought to pray that we may keep these things if we have them, or to acquire them if we do not yet have them."[32]

Augustine makes a distinction between the Good that makes us good and the good whereby we do good. "The Good which makes good is God."[33] Temporal goods are the goods whereby we do good. But they are only the material, not the cause, of moral goodness, "for though they are good in themselves they cannot make their owners good."[34] That is why they need good men to make good use of them. "Men are not made good by possessing these so-called good things, but, if men have become good otherwise, they make these things really good by using them well."[35] "Sometimes when a man has money to spare he wants to spend it on trifles. He does not dream of doing something useful with it or of laying up treasure in heaven by means of it. He is prepared to lose his money and to lose himself also together with those on whom he spends it."[36] If, on the other hand, a person is endowed with great wealth and makes good use of it, he may by so doing merit everlasting life. "If in the stewardship of temporal things we act in a manner that is just and courteous and with the moderation and sobriety befitting their nature, such conduct merits for us the rewards of eternal blessings. That is, of course, if we possess these things without being possessed by them, if they can be multiplied without entangling us, if they are made to serve us without bringing us into servitude . . . The bee has no less need of its wings when it has gathered an abundant store. If it sinks in the honey, it dies."[37]

Augustine reminds us that while eternal benefits and spiritual goods are above us, material things and temporal goods are beneath us. We are in the middle. And when we come to an age in which we are able to discern the relative worth of spiritual and material things, we must put them in their proper places, having an appreciative love for the eternal above the temporal, for the spiritual above the material. "There is a kind of human life," he writes, "that is wholly of the senses and given up to the joys of the flesh, which shuns anything which is an offense to the flesh and pursues nothing but pleasure. The happiness to be found in such a life is but transitory. It is natural to begin with this sort of life. To persist in it, however, is an act of the will. It is into this kind of life that a child is born. A child avoids so far as it can whatever it dislikes and seeks for what gives it pleasure. It is incapable of more than this. But after it has arrived at an age when the use of reason has been developed, the child can, by the help of God, choose another life the joy of which is in the mind, the happiness of which is interior and everlasting."[38]

"There has, indeed, been given to man a rational soul, but it depends on the use to which reason is put in directing the will, whether one turns to the good things of exterior nature which are the inferior or to those of his interior and higher nature. That is to say, whether one turns to the enjoyment of material and temporal things or toward that which is divine and eternal. The human soul, therefore, finds itself placed as it were in a middle ground, with material creation below it and the Creator of soul and body above it. The rational soul, then, can make a good use of material and temporal felicity provided it does not give itself over to the creature to the neglect of the Creator, of whose abounding liberality it has been bestowed. Just as all things created by God are good, from the rational creature at one end of the scale to the lowest material substance at the other, so too can the rational soul make good use of all these things, provided it be faithful to right order, and by distinguishing and choosing with discernment, set the greater things above the less, the spiritual above the corporal, the higher above the lower, the eternal above the temporal."[39]

It is made quite clear in Holy Scripture that we should not be over solicitous about material goods, and that we should not pray for them as if they were an end in themselves. *Stop worrying, then, over questions like, 'What are we to eat, or what are we to drink, or what are we to wear?' The unbelievers are always running after these things. Your heavenly Father knows all that you need. Seek first his kingship over you, his way of holiness, and all these things will be given you besides* (Matthew 6:31-33). From this text it follows that temporal goods are to be sought not in the first but in the second place; not as an end in themselves, but as a means to an end. Consequently, the Gospel injunction: *Seek first his kingship over you, his way of holiness*: "Not necessarily in order of time," explains Augustine, "but in order of importance."[40] Not all solicitude about temporal things is forbidden, therefore, but that only which is superfluous and inordinate.

Nevertheless, although we are not forbidden to love them or to seek them in moderation, we are forbidden to seek our happiness in the love of them. Material things are good in themselves but they do not make their owners good. And because they do not make them good, they cannot make them happy. "For a man can be made happy only by what makes him good."[41] Happiness is a good of the spirit and can neither be wholly bestowed nor wholly destroyed by the possession or loss of material things. Such things are to be used as a means to a higher end, not to be enjoyed for their own sake. Moreover, they are given by God as a test. If their owners use them well, they can merit greater riches in eternal life; if they use them badly, they shall neither gain eternal life nor retain the wealth bestowed on them in this life. *Tell those who are rich in this world's goods,* said Saint Paul, *not to be proud, and not to rely on so uncertain a thing as wealth. Let them trust in the God who provides us richly with all things for our use. Charge them to do good, to be rich in good works and generous, sharing what they have. Thus will they build a secure foundation for the future, for receiving that life which is life indeed* (1 Timothy 6:17-19). "God has given to men certain goods appropriate to this life . . . on the most just condition that he who rightly uses such goods will receive greater and better . . . He who uses them wrongly shall neither receive the greater nor retain the less."[42]

If material wealth made people good, Almighty God would see to it that we were all endowed with it. The fact is, however, that he bestows it on good and bad alike. Augustine tells us, "not to be dismayed by the fact that God grants such things to wicked people, for these things are of such trifling importance that they are given precisely so that we may not overvalue them. Something more than material prosperity is reserved for us. Reflect, then, on what God bestows even on the wicked, for that will give you an idea of what he reserves for the good."[43] "He who has given you everything, even your very existence, and who provides you as well as the wicked among whom you live, with sun and rain, with harvests and springs of water, with life and health and a great many comforts, he is keeping something in reserve for you that he will give only to you. And what is he reserving for you? — himself."[44]

In prayer, then, we may ask God for many things, but we must keep in mind that spiritual are to be preferred to material goods, and that the most important petition of all is for the gift of God himself. To possess God with everlasting security in a loving and happy eternity should be the final object of all our prayers. "Long for spiritual goods with all your soul," advises Augustine, "pray for them with perseverance; not with many words, but with manifest yearning. If you are always desiring, you are always praying. Ask, then, for these eternal benefits with the greatest avidity, seek them with all the energy of a strong intention, ask for them with confidence. When do you grow drowsy at prayer? When your desire grows cold. If you feel inclined to ask for temporal things, then do so in moderation, and if you receive them, rest assured that he who gives knows what is good for you."[45] If God grants them, however, he may take them away again as he did in the case of Job. But, "the spiritual things he gives you he will not take away, unless you yourself let them go."[46]

## For Our Neighbors

"If we love God we cannot despise his command to love our neighbor."[47] This precept comprises a whole series of obligations by virtue of the number and variety of persons who constitute our neighbor. The word itself signifies one who dwells near us. But Augustine would have us understand that every human being is embraced by that term.[48] Consequently, however far removed a man may be or however unknown his name, however hostile his sentiments may appear to be, it suffices that he be a man in order to be our neighbor and to have the right of appeal to our fraternal charity. Nothing is as close as a man to another man. "For every man is every man's neighbor, nor is any disparity of race to be considered where there is a common nature."[49] All men, therefore, are our neighbors, and the command of God is that we love them. We may well ask if such a love be possible considering the universality of its object. Augustine hastens to explain, saying: "All men are to be loved impartially. But since you cannot be of service to all, those are to be considered especially who, by circumstances of time or place or of certain relationships, are perhaps more closely bound to you."[50] It is obvious that we cannot apply the spiritual and corporal works of mercy to all men. But, "you should desire all men to love God together with you, and all that you do to help them or that they do to help you should be referred to that one end."[51]

Goodness is not a private good, it is a common good. It is a good which is not only not diminished by being shared, it is only possessed at all insofar as it is shared. "The possession of goodness is increased in proportion to the concord and charity of those who share it. In short, he who is unwilling to share this possession cannot have it."[52] The love of Christ for man was the desire to have sharers in his inheritance. "If we have been made sons of God we have also been made gods. But this is the effect of adoptive grace, not of a generation by nature. For only the Son of God, God, and one God with the Father, our Lord and Savior Jesus Christ, was in the beginning the Word, the Word that was with God, the Word that was God. The rest who are made gods are made by his grace, and not born of his substance that they should be the same as he, but that by favor they should come to him and be fellow heirs with Christ. Such is the love of him, the heir, that he has willed to have sharers in his heritage."[53]

The gifts of God, therefore, must not be monopolized. "It would not be right for you to close the way to godliness when you yourself have passed through."[54] To begrudge the overflowing of the gifts of God to others is unworthy of a Christian. And that is why there is such a difference between the races run in the sports arena of the world and the race of love. "In that arena, in that spectacle, *while all the runners in the stadium take part in the race,* said the Apostle Paul, *the award goes to one man* (1 Corinthians 9:24); the rest retire defeated. But in the race of love, all who run perseveringly unto the end shall be crowned together. It is charity and not competition that set this race in motion."[55] We must love our neighbor as Christ loved us, and his love for us makes us coheirs with him to the kingdom of heaven. We should desire that all men share in our good fortune. "Wherefore do I preach?" demanded Augustine. "To what end do I exist? Solely in order that not only I myself but that you also may live with Christ . . . This is my desire, my honor, my glory; this my joy, this my riches. If I preach, then, even though you do not listen, I shall still save my own soul: But I do not wish to be saved without you."[56]

We must love our neighbor as ourselves. But, "no man loves himself except he loves God."[57] He alone has a proper love of himself who loves God. "You love yourself wholesomely if you love God more than yourself. That, therefore, which you aim at in yourself, you must aim at in your neighbor, namely, that he too may love God with a love that is perfect."[58] This is love's pursuit, this the *cura dilectionis,* to transplant the love of God from one soul to another. "Through one who loves is another enflamed."[59] Augustine employs the word *rapere,* that is, to seize and carry off, to draw away to God as many as we are able. "Thus, therefore, let us love one another, and as far as we can let us by love's pursuit draw one another to have God in ourselves."[60] This, then, should be the object of our prayer for the neighbor, that he may know and love God as we know and love him ourselves. For here too prayer is the interpreter of the heart's desire; it is the expression of our love for our neighbor. "Look at the Scripture and you will find rulers commending themselves to the people's prayers. The Apostle says to his people, *Pray for us, too* (Colossians 4:3). Let all the members pray for one another, and let the head intercede for all."[61]

Before he ascended into heaven our Divine Lord said to his disciples: *You are to be my witnesses in Jerusalem, throughout Judea and Samaria, yes, even to the ends of the earth* (Acts 1:8). The commandment to love the neighbor is not to be circumscribed by the frontiers of any country; it is exceedingly broad. "Yet there are those who would set the boundaries of charity in Africa! If you would love Christ stretch out your charity over all the world, for Christ's members are spread the world over."[62] Neither, however, must our charity or our prayer be limited to those who are of the Christian faith. Augustine exhorted his people to pray for those who had not as yet received the gift of faith. He maintains that it was the prayers of the faithful, and especially the prayer of Saint Stephen, that won the gift of faith for Saul of Tarsus. "Before Saul believed, did they who had the faith pray for him or not? I have yet to learn that they did not pray for him . . . Yes, prayer was offered for him and for other unbelievers that they might believe."[63] Writing to Vitalus the Carthaginian, Augustine reminds him that the priest at the altar of God prays in a loud voice and exhorts the people to pray for those who do not believe, that God may convert them to the faith; and for catechumens, that God may inspire them with a desire for spiritual rebirth in baptism; and for the faithful also, that God may give them an increase of and perseverance in the faith.[64] Whatever the gift of God may be, it must never be monopolized. It is a common, not a private good, and the desire and prayer of a Christian must be to share it. "We pray that the Pelagians may have this gift and that our own brethren may have an increase of it. Let us not, then, be prompt in arguments and lazy in our prayers. Let us pray, dearly beloved, let us pray that the God of grace may give even to our enemies and especially to our brethren and loved ones."[65]

## For Our Enemies

We shall never understand the real meaning of Christian prayer until we have learned to love and to pray for our enemies. "What is love's perfection? To love our enemies and to love them to the end that they may be our brothers . . . Love your enemies, desiring them for brothers; love your enemies, calling them into fellowship with you."[66] Let our enemies also be drawn to God. "Draw, draw your enemy. By drawing him he will not be an enemy."[67] "It was of the perfection of love for enemies that the Lord said: *In a word, you must be made perfect as your heavenly Father is perfect* (Matthew 5:48). He, therefore, who says that he abides in him ought himself to walk as he walked. And how is that, my brethren? What does it mean to walk as Christ walked? Does it mean walking on the sea? No. It means walking the way of righteousness, and of that way I have already spoken. Nailed fast to the cross, he was walking in the way — the way of charity. *Father, forgive them, they do not know what they are doing* (Luke 23:34). So then, when you have learned to pray for your enemy, you will walk the way of the Lord."[68]

Following the example of our divine Lord, therefore, we too must pray for our enemies and not against them. Evil must never be an object of our prayers. "Let men not pray that their enemies may die, but that they may be reclaimed; then will their enmity expire and they will be enemies no longer."[69] This is what the psalmist meant when he said, *With a deadly hatred I hate them* (Psalm 139:22). That is, "I have hated their iniquities but I have loved the work of your hands, O God. This is what it means to hate with a perfect hatred: that you neither hate the man on account of the vices, nor love the vices on account of the man."[70] We must never attempt to turn God into an executioner,[71] or to make him a minister of misfortune to our enemies. That would mean casting reflection on him. "For when you call on God to destroy your enemy, or when you would take pleasure in another's misfortune and call on God to bring it about, you are trying to make him a partaker of your own malice. And, if you make him a partaker of your own malice, you call on him, not to praise him, but to cast reflection on him, for you think that God is like yourself. So is it said to you in another place, *When you do these things, shall I be deaf to it? Or do you think that I am like yourself?* (Psalm 50:21). Call on God, therefore, to praise him. Do not think that he is like unto you, so that you yourself may become like unto him."[72] "Let God please you as he is; not as you would like him to be."[73] "There is a short precept: he pleases God whom God pleases."[74]

"The Lord Jesus Christ himself loved his enemies, for as he hung upon the cross he said, *Father, forgive them; they do not know what they are doing* (Luke 23:34). Stephen followed his example when stones were being cast at him and said: *Lord, do not hold this sin against them* (Acts 7:60). The servant imitated the Lord so that no other servant might be slow to follow suit and think that this was something that could be done by the Lord alone. If, then, it be too much to imitate the Lord, let us imitate our fellow-servant."[75] "He offended those whom he was rebuking and was stoned by them. And as he was being overwhelmed by his furious persecutors and bruised to death by the stones, he first said, *Lord Jesus, receive my spirit* (Acts 7:59). Then, having prayed for himself standing, he knelt down for those who were stoning him and said, *Lord, do not hold this sin against them* — Let me die in my body, but do not let these men die in their souls. And when he had said this he fell asleep. After these words he added no more. He said them and departed. His last prayer was for his enemies."[76] We too must reach forward to this perfection of love, hoping and praying that our enemy, whoever he may be, may enjoy everlasting life together with us.[77] "So let progress be made; so let charity be cherished, that having been cherished it may become perfect; in this way the likeness of God in which you are created will be engraved anew upon your soul."[78]

## For the Dead

That Augustine believed in the efficacy of prayers for the dead is manifest from the Ninth Book of his Confessions, where he writes so beautifully of the death of his mother and asks the prayers of his readers for the repose of her soul. He quotes his mother Monica as saying, "Lay this body anywhere; let not care for it trouble you at all; this only do I ask, that you will remember me at the altar of the Lord wherever you may be."[79] He then composed the following prayer for the repose of his mother's soul: "Hearken to me through that medicine for our wounds who hung upon the tree, and who, sitting at your right hand, *makes intercession for us* (Romans 8:26). I know that from her heart she forgave her debtors; you also forgive her debts, whatever debts she may have contracted since baptism. Forgive her, O Lord, forgive her, I beseech you; *enter not into judgment with your servant* (Psalm 143:2). Let your mercy be exalted above your justice because your words are true, and you have promised mercy to the merciful . . . May she therefore rest in peace with her husband, before or after whom she married no one, whom she obeyed with patience, bringing forth fruit unto you that she might gain him also for you. And inspire, O Lord, my God, inspire your servants my brethren, your sons my masters, whom I serve with voice and heart and pen, that as many of them as shall read these Confessions may remember Monica your handmaid at your altar . . . That so my mother's last entreaty to me, may through my Confessions more than through my prayers, be more copiously fulfilled by the prayers of many others."[80]

Manifestly, his saintly mother was not worried about the place or manner of her burial. "Nothing is far to God," she was reported as saying, "nor need I fear lest he be unaware of the place whence he is to raise me up at the end of the world."[81] With her dying breath, however, she did ask Augustine to pray for her at the altar of God wherever he might be. One wonders if he recalled her last words when, twenty-seven years later (A.D. 424), he wrote *The Care of the Dead,* in reply to a query from Bishop Paulinus of Nola. Saint Paulinus had asked whether the fact of the body being buried in a holy place dedicated to some saint or martyr was of any advantage to the departed soul. Augustine replied that "although such practices are required for the consolation of men whereby they may manifest their pious regard for their departed friends, I do not see what assistance they can render to the dead; unless to this extent, that when they recall where the bodies of their loved ones lie, they may recommend to the patron saints of these places that those who have been admitted to the Lord should be assisted by their intercession."[82]

The place where bodies are interred, therefore, even though it be in holy ground, is in itself no help to the dead. If the place be dedicated to some saint or martyr, however, this may renew and increase the affectionate memory of those interceding for the dead, and cause them to seek the intercession of the saint for the souls of their departed friends.[83] Neither is the raising of a memorial or monument over the grave of any advantage to the deceased, though it may act as a memory aid to those who are bereaved. "Those things with which the graves of the dead are embellished are called memorials or monuments for no other reason than to help us to remember, and to make us think of those who have been withdrawn by death from the sight of the living, lest through forgetfulness they be withdrawn from our hearts as well. The name memorial shows this quite clearly; while a monument is so called because *moneat mentem* — it admonishes the mind."[84]

"The pomp of funerals, the crowding of funeral rites, the costly care of burial, the construction of rich monuments are solaces of a kind for the living, not aids for the dead."[85] "If an expensive funeral be of any advantage to the wicked, a cheap one or none at all would be a misfortune for the devout."[86] Nevertheless, "the bodies of the dead must not be spurned and cast aside, especially those of the good and faithful which the Holy Spirit has piously employed as instruments and vessels for every good work. For if a parent's vesture, ring, or other object of this nature be held in the greater reverence according as the parents themselves were more loved, by no means should their bodies be despised which they "wore" much more familiarly and intimately than any vesture. For our bodies are not ornaments or adjuncts that are employed externally; they pertain rather to the very nature of man."[87]

If there be question of what is really helpful to a departed soul, Augustine tells us that, "it is not to be doubted but that by the prayers of holy Church, by the saving sacrifice, and by alms expended for their souls, the dead are aided, so that the Lord should deal more mercifully with them than their sins have deserved."[88] We read in the Books of the Maccabees (2 Maccabees 12:43), that sacrifice was offered for the dead in Old Testament times. "But even if this fact were not mentioned anywhere at all in the Old Scriptures, the authority of the universal Church, which clearly sanctions this practice, is of no small account, where, in the prayers of the priest poured forth to the Lord God at his altar, a commemoration of the dead has also its proper place."[89] "Even if some necessity prevents bodies from being buried at all, or if they are not permitted to be buried in holy ground, prayers for the souls of those departed are not to be omitted, which prayers the Church undertakes to have said for all who have died in her Christian Catholic communion under a general commemoration and without mentioning their names. In this way, commemoration is made by all, for those who lack such prayers, whether of parents or children, of relatives or friends. If these supplications made with good faith and piety for the dead are unavailing, I do not think that anything else would benefit these souls, even though their lifeless bodies were laid in holy places."[90]

It follows, therefore, that even if we forget our departed dead, our holy Mother the Church does not forget them. In every sacrifice of the Mass her pious supplications are offered up so that the souls of the faithful departed may through the mercy of God rest in peace. And in the event of our remembering to pray for them we must not think that we are alone in our care for them. "Since these things are so, do not think that no help will reach the dead in whom you are interested, except that which you solemnly obtain for them by the Sacrifice of the Altar, or of prayers or almsgiving. These, indeed, may not benefit all for whom you offer them, but only those who while here on earth so lived as to obtain benefit from them."[91] For there is one thing we must always remember about the souls of the faithful departed, and it is this, that their degree of merit was fixed the moment they died. They can no longer merit anything because progress by means of personal and meritorious effort is a law of this life, not of the next.

Souls that have departed from this life, therefore, cannot help themselves, but we can help them by our prayers. Nevertheless, the benefits that may come to them through such prayers depend on whether they themselves merited such benefits while on earth. "It cannot be denied," declares Augustine, "that the souls of the dead are benefited by the piety of their living friends who offer the Sacrifice of the Mediator or give alms in the Church on their behalf. But these services are of advantage to those only who, during their lives, have earned such merit that services of this kind can help them. For there is a manner of life that is neither so good as not to require these services after death, nor so bad that such services are of no avail. On the other hand, there is a manner of life so good as not to require them, and again, there is one so bad that when life is over they render no help."[92]

"Therefore, it is in this life that all merit or demerit is acquired which can alleviate or aggravate a man's sufferings after this life. No man need hope, then, that after he is dead he shall obtain merit with God which he neglected to secure here. Accordingly, it is manifest that the services which the Church celebrates for the dead are in no way opposed to the words of the Apostle: *The lives of all of us are to be revealed before the tribunal of Christ so that each one may receive his recompense, good or bad, according to his life in the body* (2 Corinthians 5:10). For the merits that make such services as I speak of profitable to a man are earned while he is *in the body* . . . Therefore, when sacrifices either of the altar or of alms are offered on behalf of all the baptized dead, they are thank offerings for the very good; propitiatory offerings for the not very bad; and in the case of the very bad — a kind of consolation for the living."[93]

Augustine makes it quite clear, however, that it is not within our competency to judge the souls of the dead or to decide which souls may or may not be profitably prayed for. "Since you cannot distinguish who these are," he says, "it behooves you to intercede for all those who have been regenerated, so that none may be omitted who can and who ought to benefit by these suffrages. For it is better that they should superabound for those whom they neither hurt nor help, than that they be wanting to those who need them."[94] As far as the burial of the dead is concerned, let us remember that "whatever the service performed over a body to be interred, such service is not a guarantee of salvation, but an office of humanity performed in response to the feeling that no one bears enmity toward his own flesh.[95] Wherefore, it behooves us, inasmuch as we are able, to have a care for the body of our neighbor when he who formerly cared for it has departed this life. For if they who have no faith in the resurrection do such things, how much more ought we who believe in that doctrine, so that a duty of this nature performed over a dead body — which will yet rise again and continue for eternity — may also in some manner bear witness to that belief?"[96]

"Permit me, O Lord, to indulge in a reasonable amount of grief at the passing of my loved ones, and let me pour forth my tears in sorrow so consoling to our human nature — tears quickly dried by the gladness of faith whereby I believe that when the faithful leave us in death, they only precede us for a time to seek the enjoyments of a better life . . . According to my means I shall provide for the obsequies of my deceased friends and shall erect monuments to their memory. For when such things were performed, not only over the bodies of the prophets and of other saints, but over human bodies wherever lying, they were accounted as good works in Holy Scripture, and they, furthermore, who performed these rights over your own body were praised and acclaimed by men. I shall fulfill these offices for my dear departed ones as my final duty toward them and as a balm to my own aching heart. And moreover, I, who not only carnally but spiritually loved my dear ones — now dead to me in body but not in spirit — will faithfully, regularly, and frequently procure for them those blessings which never fail to succor the souls of the departed, namely, Masses, prayers, and alms-deeds."[97]

"The blessed Apostle admonishes us that *We would have you be clear about those who sleep in death, brothers* — that is, concerning our dead and dearest ones — *otherwise you might yield to grief, like those who have no hope* (1 Thessalonians 4:13), the hope, namely, of resurrection and of everlasting incorruptibility. Therefore does the truest use of Scripture refer to them as sleeping, so that when we hear of their sleeping we may by no means despair of their waking again . . . The Apostle, then, did not admonish us not to be sorrowful, but not to mourn *like those who have no hope.* We are sorrowful at the death of our friends because of the necessity of losing them, but always with the hope of recovering them"[98] "Perish, then, the grief of the Gentiles who are without hope! I can be sad, but when I mourn I am comforted by hope. And away with sorrow since so much consolation abounds! Let grief be blotted from the heart; let faith chase sorrow away. Grief ill becomes the temple of God where there is so much hope. There dwells the sweet consoler; there dwells one ever faithful to his promises."[99]

Augustine tells us that he himself felt the gentle touch of the Great Consoler when, awakening from sleep on the morning following his mother's burial, he felt his grief "not a little mitigated."[100] And as he lay there, the words of a poem by Saint Ambrose came to his mind:

O God, the world's great architect,
Who does heaven's rowling orbs direct;
Clothing the day with beauteous light,
And with sweet slumbers silent night;
When wearied limbs new vigor gain,
From rest, new labors to sustain;
When hearts oppressed do meet relief,
And anxious minds forget their grief.[101]

CHAPTER 5

# HOW WE SHOULD PRAY

## Prayer Should Come From the Heart

PRAYER IS THE AFFECTIONATE reaching out of the mind for God. It is the articulation of the pilgrim's desire for God and for the eternal happiness which God has promised to those who love him. "For something is promised which we do not yet possess, but because he who has promised is true, we rejoice in hope, and because we have not received what he has promised, we sigh with yearning."[1] This yearning of the heart is our prayer, so prayer must come from the heart. And since our prayer is the expression of our heart's desire, it follows that prayer is an internal rather than an external operation. "Prayer is a spiritual thing," says Augustine, "and the truer it is to its nature the more pleasing it is to God."[2] It can never be just a matter of words. Prayer is the language of love. "Let there be earnest affection in prayer and the effectual answer of him who hears it will be realized."[3] "If you knock with pious affection and with sincere heartfelt love, he who sees from what motive you knock will open unto you."[4]

As we have seen, prayer has a voice of its own, quite apart from the voice of the one who prays. "Crying to God is not done with the physical voice, but with the heart. Many whose lips are silent cry out with the heart; many are noisy with their mouths but with their hearts averted are able to obtain nothing. If, then, you cry to God, cry out inwardly where he hears you."[5] The voice of prayer is the voice of the heart's desire. Let us recall, however, that Augustine uses the term "heart" in a scriptural sense. For him it signifies — as it does in many passages of Scripture — our whole interior and spiritual life, and it includes mind and will, knowledge and love. Knowledge founded on faith, whereby we believe that God hears and answers us; love, which grows and expands through hope in the benefactor from whom we await a favorable answer. Mind and will, faith, hope, and charity, all are called into play in the activity of prayer. "Let the inner man, therefore, in whom Christ has begun to live by faith, cry unto the Lord, not with the voice of his lips, but with the affection of his heart. God does not hear as man hears, for unless you cry with the noise of the lungs and tongue a man does not hear you, but your thought is your cry to the Lord."[6]

Speaking on the eighty-fifth psalm Augustine puts these words on the lips of the Savior: "Do you desire that I would fix your prayer in my ears? Then, fix my law in your heart."[7] It is for this reason that Augustine insists so much upon the need of purifying our hearts. If the heart be full of sinful desires, the soul becomes cramped for space and there is no room for God. "Cramped is the dwelling of my soul," he lamented in his Confessions. "Expand it that you may enter in. It is in ruins; restore it. There is that about it which must offend your eyes; I know it and I confess it. But who will cleanse it? To whom shall I cry but to you?"[8]

"Blessed are they who rejoice when they enter their own hearts and find nothing evil there . . . And that you may be able to return willingly to your own heart, purify it: *Blest are the single-hearted for they shall see God* (Matthew 5:8). From there take away evil desires, take away the taint of avarice, take away the plague of superstition, take away sacrilege and evil thoughts, hatred also, and, I say, not only against a friend but against an enemy. Take away all these things, then enter into your heart and you shall rejoice in it, for the very cleanness of your heart shall delight you and make you pray. Just as when you come to any place where there is silence and quiet and where the place is clean, you say, 'Let us pray here,' because the quietness of the place delights you, and you believe that God will hear you there. If, then, the visible cleanliness of a place delights you, how is it that the uncleanness of your heart does not offend you? Enter in, clean it up, lift up your eyes to God, and immediately he will hear you."[9] *The Lord is near to all who call upon him* (Psalm 145:18) declared the psalmist. "But see what follows," remarks Augustine. "He is near *to all who call upon him in truth.* For many call upon him, but not in truth. They seek somthing else from him, but not himself."[10]

God must be our first love, and this should find honest expression in our prayers. "Woe to that love of yours if you can conceive anything more beautiful than him from whom is all beauty, anything to keep you back from deserving to think of him."[11] "God would have himself gratuitously worshipped, would have himself gratuitously loved, that is, chastely loved, not to be loved for the reason that he gives anything beside himself, but because he gives himself."[12] Prayer should come from the heart, from a heart that is right with God. "The heart is right with God when it seeks God for the sake of God."[13] The seventy-seventh psalm speaks of a *wayward and rebellious* generation that had sought God in prayer solely for the sake of material gain. "They were loving with their lips and lying with their tongues, but at heart they were not right with God, as long as they preferred those things for the sake of which they required the help of God."[14]

"Hope for nothing else from the Lord your God, but let the Lord your God himself be your hope. Many people hope to obtain riches from God, and many hope for perishable and transitory honors. In short, they hope to get at God's hands anything else, except only God himself. See to it that you seek after God himself, nay, more, despise other things and make your way to him. Forget other things, remember him. Leave other things behind and reach forward to him. It was he assuredly who set you right when turned away from the right path. He it is who is leading you to your goal. Therefore, let him be your hope who is guiding and leading you to your destination."[15] "For we cultivate God, and God cultivates us. But we do not cultivate God so as to make him any better by so doing. Our cultivation is the labor of an adoring heart, not of the hands. He cultivates us as the husbandman tills his field. In cultivating us he makes us better just as the husbandman by tilling his field makes it better. And the fruit he seeks in us is that we may cultivate him. The tillage he practices on us is that he never ceases to root out the evil seeds from our hearts by his word, to open our hearts, as it were, by the plough of his word, to plant the seed of his precepts and to wait for the fruit of piety. For when we have received that tillage in our hearts so as to cultivate him well, we are not ungrateful to our husbandman, but yield the fruit wherein he delights. And our fruit does not make him the richer, but it makes us all the happier."[16]

## Prayer Should Be for Salvation

Augustine maintains that a man is what his love makes him and that he is virtuous insofar as he loves what ought to be loved. It is the quality of his love which also determines the quality and the efficacy of his prayer. To love and to possess God in the everlasting security of eternal life should be the final object of all our prayers. "Understand, then, brethren, that every believer who has the word of God in his heart, . . . asks for many things 'according to this world' and is not heard, but when he asks for life eternal he is always heard."[17] The reason being, of course, that such prayer is made in the name of the Savior. *Anything you ask me in my name I will do* (John 14:14), declared our Divine Lord. *I go to the Father, and whatever you ask in my name I will do so as to glorify the Father in the Son* (John 14:13). "Wake up, then, man of faith, and hear attentively what is said there: *in my name.* And what is he called who promised so great a benefit? Why, he is called Christ Jesus. Christ means King; Jesus means Savior . . . Wherefore, when we wish that he would do whatever we ask, let us not ask as if it did not matter how we asked, but let us ask in his name, in the name of the Savior. Let us not ask, therefore, contrary to salvation."[18] "When we ask properly, let us ask him not to grant what we ask improperly."[19]

*Until now,* said the Savior, *you have asked for nothing in my name. Ask and you shall receive, that your joy may be full* (John 16:24). "We know that what he terms full joy is not carnal but spiritual joy, and when it will be so great that nothing can be added to it, no doubt it will then be full. Whatever is asked, therefore, that has reference to this joy, is to be asked in the name of Christ; that is, if we understand the grace of God and desire a truly happy life. To ask anything else is to ask nothing. Not that any other thing would be actually nothing, but that in comparison to so great a thing, whatever else is desired is comparatively nothing . . . That the faithful should ask, therefore, not for nothing, but for full joy, that is what he exhorts, saying, *Ask and you shall receive, that your joy may be full.* That is, ask in my name that your joy may be full and you shall receive it."[20]

The full joy of neverending life, love, and happiness and the means to secure them — these are the objects of the pilgrim's prayer and they are the gifts of God. Consequently, we must ask for them. And we shall not ask with any degree of fervor or sincerity unless we really do desire them. It is not enough merely to acknowledge the worthiness of these objects — we must love them, we must want them. "It does not follow that we shall strive for that which we have recognized as worth our striving, unless we delight in it in the measure in which it should be loved."[21] This pleasure and delight in goodness is the effect of grace. No man gives "delight in the Lord" to himself; it is only the Lord who gives sweetness. *No one can come to me unless the Father who sent me draws him* (John 6:44). Preaching on these words Augustine explains that this "drawing" by the Father is a "violence done to the heart." But we must not suppose that it is "a rough or uneasy kind of violence." No. "It is gentle, it is sweet; it is the very sweetness of it that draws you."[22]

Speaking on the thirtieth psalm, Augustine praises the psalmist who, by God's grace, composed and sang this prayer-song of a longing heart. "The subject of song and of praise in this psalm, is the City whose citizens we are, insofar as we are Christians; the City from which we are absent as long as we are mortal; the City to which we are going: through the approaches to which . . . the Sovereign of the City has made himself the way for us to reach it. Walking thus in Christ, pilgrims until we arrive, sighing as we yearn for a certain ineffable repose that dwells within that City, a repose of which it has been promised that *eye has not seen, ear has not heard, nor has it so much as dawned on man what God has prepared for those who love him* (1 Corinthians 2:9), so doing, let us sing the song of a longing heart. He who truly yearns sings that song in hs soul even though his tongue be silent. He who does not sing it is voiceless before God, however much he may sound in the ears of men. See what ardent lovers of that City were they by whom these words were composed and handed down to us! With how deep a feeling were they sung by them; a feeling that the love of that City created in them; a love inspired by the Spirit of God!"[23]

Eternal Life, in which God himself is to be enjoyed, is the motive of all Christian life and worship. Christians flock to their churches in order to hear "how they must live well in this present time, so that after this life they may deserve to live happily and forever."[24] They worship God gratis, "desiring from him not the visible rewards of service, not felicity in this present time, but eternal life alone, in which God himself is to be enjoyed . . . For then is the Law also fulfilled, when all God's commandments are performed not in the covetous desire of temporal things, but for the love of him who commanded them."[25] "For God is to be loved freely, and the soul cannot rest save in that which it loves. But eternal rest is given to it only in the love of God, who alone is eternal."[26] "Nothing that God can promise is of any worth apart from God himself."[27] "He who has given the promise is himself the end of our longing. He will give himself because he has given himself. He will give his own immortal being to our immortality because he gave himself as mortal to our mortality."[28] He is the reward of our love and of our worship — "It is he whom we long to receive who makes us ask; it is he whom we hope to find who makes us seek . . ."[29]

*If you live in me, and my words stay part of you,* said the Savior, *you may ask what you will — it will be done for you* (John 15:7). "Abiding in Christ, how can they ask anything but what becomes Christ?" demands Augustine. "How can they wish anything while abiding in the Savior but what is not alien to salvation? But we wish one thing because we are in this world, and sometimes, because of our abiding in this world, the thought steals into our minds of asking for something which we do not realize to be inexpedient for us. But God forbid it should be done for us if we abide in Christ who, when we ask, does only what is good for us. Abiding, therefore, in him while his word abides in us, we shall ask what we will and it shall be done for us . . . And then may his words be said to abide in us when we do the things he commands us and love the things he has promised us."[30] The aim of all Christian endeavor is "to think on God and to love him, to love freely the God who is our helper, who watches our striving, who crowns our victory, who bestows the prize — in fine, to count God himself the prize, to expect nothing from him but himself. If you love, love freely: If you love in truth, let him whom you love be your reward."[31]

## Prayer Should Be Forgiving

If there be one thing Augustine insists upon, it is that we must speak the truth when we pray. That fair words may hide an ugly disposition is common enough experience. Scripture tells us that words are the heart's overflow. Provided, of course, they are not spoken by a hypocrite. There is no deception in nature. Good fruit comes from a good tree, bad fruit comes from a bad tree. But man is so constituted that even pious formulas of prayer may come from a lying heart. Consequently, if we wish our prayer to be effective, we must speak the truth when we pray. That is, if we expect God to give and to forgive, we on our part must forgive and give to our neighbor. "There are two works of mercy which deliver us and which the Lord himself laid down briefly in the Gospel: *Pardon, and you shall be pardoned. Give, and it shall be given to you* (Luke 6:37-38). Pardon and you shall be pardoned refers to forgiving; give and it shall be given you refers to doing kindnesses. With regard to what he said concerning pardon, you wish your own sin to be forgiven and you are willing to forgive another. Again, as far as doing kindnesses is concerned, a beggar asks of you and you yourself are God's beggarman. We are all God's beggarmen when we pray."[32] To forgive those who have injured or offended us is a necessary condition of effective prayer. "He who is not willing to pardon his brother must not expect an answer to his prayers."[33]

"Let no man, therefore, refuse to forgive, lest his own sin be retained against him when he prays. For God says, *Pardon, and you shall be pardoned,* that is, I have first forgiven you, do you at least forgive after that. If you will not forgive, I will call you back, and I will put upon you all I have remitted to you . . . *My heavenly*

*Father will treat you in exactly the same way unless each of you forgives his brother from his heart* (Matthew 18:35). Do not say, 'I forgive' with the tongue and neglect to forgive in the heart, for by his threat of vengeance God shows you your punishment. God knows where you speak. Man hears your voice, God looks into your conscience. If you say, 'I forgive,' then do so. It is better that you be violent in speech and forgive in your heart, than that you be soft in speech and relentless at heart."[34]

Prayer must be accompanied by good works; it must have two wings — the giving of alms and the forgiving of injuries. "Do all that you can," counsels Augustine, "do it by every means at your command, do it cheerfully, and so send up your prayer with confidence. It will have two wings: a double alms. And what is the double alms? *Pardon, and you shall be pardoned. Give, and it shall be given to you* (Luke 6:37-38). One of these alms is that which is done from the heart when you forgive your brother his offenses; the other is what you give out of your possessions when you give bread to the poor. Offer both, for fear that without either wing your prayer remain motionless."[35] "Scorn not the one who entreats you, and when you cannot grant his request, at least do not spurn him. If you can, give; if you are unable to give, be affable. God crowns the interior desire when he finds not the ability to give. Let no one say, 'I have nothing.' Charity is not doled out of a bag. For whatever we say or have said or shall ever be able to say, either we ourselves or those after us or those before us, we have no end but charity. For *what we are aiming at in this warning is the love that springs from a pure heart, a good conscience, and sincere faith* (1 Timothy 1:5)."[36]

"Question your own hearts when you pray to God, and see how you utter that verse, *Forgive us the wrong we have done as we forgive those who wrong us* (Matthew 6:12). You will not be praying unless you say that. If you say any other prayer he does not hear you, because it is not the one which the advocate sent by him dictated. It is necessary, therefore, even when we use our own words in prayer, that we pray after the manner of that prayer, and when we use the very words of that prayer it is not necessary that we have a right understanding of it, for God willed that it should be clear. If, therefore, you will not pray, you have no hope. If you pray in some manner other than that which the Master taught you or if you are false in your prayer, you will not be heard. Therefore, you must pray, you must speak the truth when you pray, and you must pray as he taught you. Whether you mean what you say or not, you will be saying every day, *Forgive us the wrong we have done as we forgive those who wrong us.* Would you say this without fear? Then, do what you say."[37]

If the question arises as to how often one should forgive, one recalls that Simon Peter himself asked that question, inquiring specifically if seven times would be sufficient. The Lord answered him: *No, not seven times; I say, seventy times seven times* (Matthew 18:22). And what is the meaning of seventy times seven times? According to Augustine it means simply seventy-seven times. Does this mean that if someone offends me seventy-eight times, I need not forgive him? "No," answers Augustine, "I dare say that if he should sin against you seventy-eight times, you must forgive him . . . And if he sins a hundred times, forgive him. Why need I say how often? In a word, as often as he shall sin, forgive him. Have I, then, taken upon myself to overstep the measure of my Lord? Oh, no, I have not at all presumed to go beyond that. I have heard the Lord speaking to his Apostle in a passage where neither measure nor number is fixed: For he says, *Forgive whatever grievances you have against one another. Forgive as the Lord has forgiven you* (Colossians 3:13)."[38]

"Here you have the rule. If Christ has forgiven your sins seventy-seven times only and has refused to pardon beyond that, then you also may fix that limit and refuse to go beyond it. But if Christ has found thousands of sins on top of sins and has nevertheless forgiven them all, then do not you withdraw your mercy but grant the forgiveness of that great number. It was not without meaning that the Lord said, *seventy times seven,* for there is no offense whatever which you ought not to forgive . . . So let us be willing and ready to forgive all trespasses committed against us, if we ourselves desire to be forgiven . . . Therefore, do we daily beg, daily prostrate ourselves and say: *Forgive us the wrong we have done as we forgive those who wrong us.* What debts of yours?

All of them or just a certain number? All of them, you say. Then, you do likewise with your debtor. This, then, is the rule you lay down, this is the condition you speak of, this is the covenant and agreement you enter into when you pray, saying, *Forgive us the wrong we have done as we forgive those who wrong us.*"[39]

If this quality of forgiveness were characteristic of our prayer, then our prayers would have an incalculable community value, the effect of which would be apparent in mutual forbearance at all times and in a happier social relationship with those around us. "If anyone should have offended another by harshly reproaching, abusing, or calumniating him, he should make amends at the earliest possible opportunity, and he who has been injured should pardon the offense without further controversy. If, however, the injury has been mutual, the obligation on both parties and the effect of their prayers should be mutual forgiveness, for the more frequent your prayers, the greater should be their efficacy in healing discord."[40]

## Prayer Should Be Humble

*And to some who trusted in themselves as just and despised others, he spoke also this parable: Two men went up to the temple to pray; one was a Pharisee, the other a tax collector. The Pharisee with head unbowed prayed in this fashion: I give you thanks, O God, that I am not like the rest of men — grasping, crooked, adulterous — or even like this tax collector. I fast twice a week; I pay tithes on all I possess* (Luke 18:10-12). Such was the Pharisee's prayer. Augustine remarked that he might at least have moderated his claim and said that he was not like a good many other people. But no. He had to be absolutely unique. Scripture compares this type of person to the unicorn, which is a fabulous, prancing beast, having the head, neck, and body of a horse, the legs of a deer, the tail of a lion, and a single horn in the center of its forehead. "For pride hates companionship, and every proud man strives with all his might to shine alone."[41] He is so full of himself and his own righteousness that he stands in need of nothing — not even from God. The Pharisee was so right in his own conceit that he had no petition whatever to place before the Lord. "In all his words you may look for any single thing he asked of God and you will not find it. He went up to pray, yet he had no mind to pray, but rather to praise himself. Indeed, it is only a small part of it that he did not pray but rather praised himself; he even mocked the one who did pray."[42]

*The other man, however, kept his distance* (Luke 18:13). "Hear still more about the humility of the tax collector. It is but a small matter that he stood afar off, *not even daring to raise his eyes to heaven.* He did not dare look upwards; his conscience pressed him down, though his hope raised him upwards . . . *All he did was beat his breast and say: O God, be merciful to me, a sinner.* You have heard the case of the Pharisee and the tax collector, now hear the sentence. You have heard the proud accuser, you have heard the humble criminal. Now hear the Judge . . . *Believe me, this man went home from the temple justified but the other did not* . . . You have heard the sentence. Beware, then, of pride."[43] The Pharisee praised himself. The tax collector praised God, for by his confession and plea for mercy, he acknowledged that only God could raise him from the death of sin. Consequently, he was justified rather than the other. "Do you wish to reach God with your prayer? Then, humble yourself . . . Have humility in your heart and God will exalt you. He will come to you and take up his abode with you."[44]

If the humility of God-made-man was the cause of profound wonder to Augustine, so also was the conceit of proud men who refuse to confess their sins, who attribute whatever good they to do themselves, and who despise others whom they esteem as less worthy than themselves.[45] For Augustine, man owes his very being to God. Everything from this life to eternal life is God's gift to man. Faith, hope, charity; knowledge and love; pleasure and delight in doing good; yes, even prayer itself, all are the gifts of God. What has man that he has not received? Why does he boast as if he had not received it? To the proud man Almighty God says: "Not you, but I, am God. I created, I re-create; I formed, I re-form; I made, I re-make; if you could not make yourself, how can you re-make yourself?"[46] "Away with you, away with you, I say, from yourself," exhorts Augustine. "You only hinder yourself. If you build yourself you build a ruin. *Unless the Lord build the house, they labor in vain who build it* (Psalm 126:1)."[47] "This, then, is the Christian theory: No man does anything well but by the grace of God. What a man does ill is his own doing: what he does well is of God's bounty. When he begins to do well let him not attribute it to himself; rather let him give thanks to him from whom he has received it."[48]

God made man. Man made sin. The Son of God came to destroy what man made, to redeem and save what God made. In so doing he traced out for man to follow a way in which the spirit of humility was most divinely exemplified. "It was not possible for this spirit to be produced in us by any means at once more glorious or more gentle — subduing our pride, as it does, by persuasion rather than by violence — than that the Word . . . should condescend so to reveal and exercise his personality in human form, as to make man more afraid of being exalted by the pride of man, than of being humbled after the example of God."[49] "He lies in the manger, but contains the world; . . . he is wrapped in swaddling clothes, but vests us with immortality; . . . he found no place at the inn, but makes for himself a temple in the hearts of those who believe in him."[50] "He cried in the manger in wordless infancy; he, the Word, without whom all human eloquence is mute."[51] "What pride can be cured if it be not cured by the humility of the Son of God?"[52] "The Son of God was humiliated for you. It may be that you are ashamed to imitate a humble man; at least, then, imitate a humble God."[53] "That which he became for your sake is what you must attend to in him if you would be like him."[54]

*The Word became flesh and made his dwelling among us* (John 1:14). He condescended to share our mortality so that he might raise us up to a participation in his divinity. *You are well acquainted with the favor shown you by our Lord Jesus Christ: how for your sake he made himself poor though he was rich, so that you might become rich by his poverty* (2 Corinthians 8:9). But mortality is the disease from which all men die. It is the punishment of that pride which made man think he could be like God. To heal this pride the Son of God humbly assumed our mortality and pledged himself obedient to death — even unto the death of the cross. At least, then, let man acknowledge his mortality. Let him accept it humbly as the punishment due to sin, acknowledging its shortcomings and its imperfections. Why is he proud? He cannot give himself even this mortality in which he dies! His pride, in a sense, is worse than that of Lucifer. "O haughty mortal! Compared with the devil you should blush for shame. Though proud, he is immortal; though malignant, he is a spirit."[55] "Man, acknowledge that you are a man. All your humility depends upon your knowledge of yourself."[56]

In spite of his mortality, however, man seeks the immortal. His death-environed spirit was made for God and shall know no rest until it rests in him. He seeks everlasting life, everlasting health, everlasting happiness, and these benefits depend upon the immortality that only God can bestow. No man gives them to himself. There is no doubt as to what answer Augustine would have given to the question: Can man do without God? If man seeks to be emancipated from God, he seeks an impossible independence. "For that we shall be just from being unjust, strong from being weak, alive from being dead, immortal from being mortal, happy from being miserable, is of his mercy."[57] If man seeks everlasting life, love, and happiness, he must humbly hope in God to receive them. *Cursed is the man who trusts in human beings* (Jeremiah 17:5). "Therefore, do not hope in yourself for you too are a man. If you place your hope in another man you are dangerously proud."[58] "This, then, is the first grace of God's gift, to bring us to the confession of our weakness, that whatever good we can do, whatever our ability may be, we may be that in him, so that *let him who would boast, boast in the Lord* (1 Corinthians 1:31)."[59]

Our humility, moreover, must not be just a pious sentiment or a mere formula of words; it must be an intellectual conviction. "For then shall humility be sincere, if it be not merely professed with the tongue . . ."[60] We must say it in the heart where God hears it. We must acknowledge our need and be convinced of our radical incapacity to reach our supernatural end without the aid of God. "One man is wealthy in money and is proud on that score; another is wealthy in honors and is proud for that reason; another thinks himself to be wealthy in righteousness and hence his pride.

Which is worse . . . But humility goes along with confession, the humility whereby we confess ourselves to be sinners."[61] Pride praises itself; humility praises God and prays for mercy. *Incline your ear, O Lord; answer me, for I am afflicted and poor* (Psalm 86:1). "The rich man, then, he does not bow down his ear, but to the poor, to the one that is in misery, that is, to the humble; to the one who confesses, to the one who is in need of mercy. But not to the one who is full, who lifts himself up, who boasts as if he wanted nothing — who says, *I give you thanks, O God, that I am not like . . . this tax collector* — for the rich Pharisee boasted of his merits; the poor tax collector confessed his sins."[62]

## Prayer Should Be Attentive

Prayer is the affectionate reaching out of the mind for God and, consequently, demands attention to God. Now, if the mind be preoccupied with the thought of God, there is no difficulty about attention at prayer. It is only when the mind is more concerned about temporal things than it is about God that proper attention at prayer becomes a problem. Then, it may issue an order to itself to pay attention to God and find that the order is not being obeyed. "The nature of the soul is more excellent than the nature of the body; it far surpasses it; it is a spiritual thing, incorporeal. It rules the body, moves the limbs, guides the senses; it prepares ideas, puts forth action, takes in images of countless things. Who is there, in short, who can adequately praise the soul?"[63] We find an order issued to the soul, and the order is not issued by the body, which is inferior to the soul and cannot issue orders to its superior. So the command comes from the soul exhorting itself to fidelity in the praise of God. "For . . . she perceives that certain inferior parts of her are disturbed by worldly emotions and by a certain excitement of earthly desires, so that they turn themselves to outward things away from God who is within. So she recalls herself from outward to inward things, from lower to higher things, and says: 'Praise the Lord, O my soul.' "[64]

However, it is one thing to issue an order and quite another thing to have that order obeyed. "The mind gives the body an order and is obeyed at once; the mind gives itself an order and is resisted. The mind commands the hand and there is such readiness that you can hardly distinguish the command from its execution . . . The mind commands the mind to will . . . but it does not do so . . . The mind, I say, commands the mind to will — it would not give the command unless it willed — yet the order is not obeyed. The trouble is that it does not totally command. It commands insofar as it wills, and it disobeys the command insofar as it does not will . . . But it does not give the command in its fullness and, consequently, is not obeyed."[65]

This seems to indicate the need of very determined and strongminded action. Yet, in writing to the Lady Proba on the subject of prayer, Augustine remarks that attention should never be forced. He maintains that prayer should be shortened to suit the capacity of the soul, rather than that the soul be forced to do something it cannot continue over a long period. "The brethren in Egypt," he writes, "are reported to have very frequent and very brief prayers. Their prayers are, as it were, quick and ejaculatory, for fear the wide-awake conscious attention so indispensable in prayer should vanish or lose its keenness by prolonged exercises. And in this they show plainly enough that just as this attention should not be allowed to exhaust itself if it cannot continue for long, so neither should it be suddenly suspended if it be sustained. Far be it from us to speak too much in prayer or to refrain from prolonged prayer if fervent attention of soul continue. To employ much speaking in prayer is to use a superfluity of words in asking a necessary thing, but to prolong prayer is to have the soul throbbing with continued pious emotion toward him to whom we pray."[66]

God is the aim of our prayer; he should be the goal of all our desires. He wants our minds and hearts to be set on him alone. And the purpose of having definite times for prayer and of using words when we pray is to fix our attention on our desires, to direct them deliberately toward God, to construct them on spiritual lines and, as it were, to lift them up off the earth. "If you had corn in your rooms below, you would take it up higher for fear it should rot. Would you remove your corn and let your heart rot on the earth? You would take your corn up higher; then lift your heart up to heaven. Do you ask, how can I? What ropes are needed? What machinery? What ladders? Your affections are the steps; your will is the way. By loving, you ascend; by neglecting, you descend. Standing on the earth you are in heaven if you love God. For the heart is not raised as the body is raised. For the body to be raised, it changes its place; for the heart to be raised, it changes its desire."[67]

Prayer must come from the heart; it is not just a mechanical operation. In his *Rule,* Augustine says: "Ponder in your hearts the meaning of the psalms and hymns your voices raise to God."[68] If the words we use in prayer, therefore, give expression to sentiments of joy or sorrow, of love and devotion, of compunction or of the holy fear of God, we must enter into these sentiments with all our hearts. "If the psalm prays, do you also pray: if it laments, so do you too lament; if it gives thanks, give thanks with it; if it hopes, so you too; if it speaks in accents of fear, so do you also tremble with it. For all that is written there is meant to be a mirror for us."[69]

No doubt we would all like to pray in this wholehearted, concentrated fashion. But how often are our prayers rendered ineffective by distractions? "Brethren," says Augustine, "let me speak to you as a man to his fellowmen. I want each one of you to look into his own heart now and to study himself without either flattery or deception, for nothing could be more foolish than for a man either to flatter or to deceive himself. Let us examine and see what goes on in a man's heart. Note, for instance, that our very prayers are constantly hindered by idle thoughts, so that one's mind can hardly concentrate upon God. True, we do wish to be steadfastly occupied with the thought of him, but somehow or other the mind seems to elude itself. It seeks in vain for some fence that will shut it in, for something to check its idle flittings to and fro, so that it may find happiness in God without distraction. Yet, how rarely, in spite of our many prayers, do we pray in such a manner?"[70]

"Behold, a man stands up and sings to God at great length, and frequently his lips are moving in song while his thoughts are flitting through I know not what desires. Our minds, then, stood up as it were to praise God; our souls meanwhile were drifting hither and thither amid various desires or business anxieties. The mind observes it from above, drifting this way and that, and turning, as it were, to the soul disturbed by anxieties, it says: 'Praise the Lord, O my soul.' Why busy yourself with other things? Why are you taken up with anxieties about things of the earth and of this life? Stand with me and praise the Lord."[71] "Why," he asks, "do we praise the Lord so imperfectly and with so little persistence? Because *the corruptible body burdens the soul and the earthen shelter weighs down the mind that has many concerns* (Wisdom 9:15). Oh, take from me this body that weighs down the soul and then I will praise the Lord; take from me this earthly habitation that presses down the mind musing upon many things. Then will I gather myself into one compact whole and praise the Lord."[72]

Some people think that they themselves are the only ones afflicted with distractions at prayer, and to these Augustine gives consolation and encouragement: consolation, by reminding them that even King David found it difficult to make his fugitive heart stand still to praise the Lord; encouragement, by reminding them that the Lord to whom they pray is sweet and mild in putting up with imperfect prayers and that he patiently awaits the prayer that will be perfect. "Each one might say that this happened only to himself but not to others if he did not find David in Holy Scripture praying in a certain place, saying: *Therefore your servant now finds the courage to make this prayer to you* (2 Samuel 7:27). He said that he had found his heart, as if it were accustomed to run away from him. He chased his fugitive heart and, being unable to catch it, cried to God, saying: 'For my heart has deserted me.' "[73]

*Gladden the soul of your servant, for to you, O Lord, I lift up my soul, for you, O Lord, are good and forgiving, abounding in kindness to all who call upon you* (Psalm 86:4-5). "I think I see what he means by forgiving," says Augustine. "I feel that he calls God forgiving for this reason, that he bears with those failings of ours and yet expects prayer from us in order to make us perfect. And when we have given it to him, he receives it gratefully and listens to it and does not remember the many prayers we poured out without thinking, but accepts the one that we can hardly find. For what man is there, my brethren, who on being addressed by his friend, and wishing to answer him, sees him turn away and speak to another — what man will put up with this? Or if you appeal to a judge and set him up to hear you, and all at once, when you are speaking to him, you turn away and begin to converse with a friend — who will endure such conduct? Yet God puts up with the hearts of so many people who pray yet think of other things. I am not now speaking of evil things that are perverse and at enmity with God, but to think of anything that is superfluous is an offense to him with whom you had begun to speak. Your prayer is a conversation with God. When you read, God speaks to you; when you pray, you speak to God."[74]

"If you were speaking with me and were suddenly to turn away to your servant and leave me — I do not say merely in the event of your asking something of me, but even speaking to me as an equal — would I not think that an insult had been offered to me? Yet, that is what you do to God everyday."[75] "But what are we to say? Are we to despair of the human race and say that everyone who suffers from distractions is damned? Were we to say that, brethren, I fail to see what hope would be left for any of us."[76] While commenting on this same psalm,, Augustine composed the following homely prayer: " 'For you, O Lord, are sweet and mild.' Mild, that is, in putting up with me. Because of my infirmity I wander. Cure me and I shall stand firm; strengthen me and I shall be strong. But until you do, put up with me, for you, O Lord, are sweet and mild."[77]

## Prayer Should Be Constant

Prayer is the expression of a desire, and it will not be effective unless the desire is strong enough to make us persevere in asking. Seldom has our Divine Lord spoken with such emphasis as when enjoining constancy in prayer. "We have heard him in the Gospel exhorting us to ask insistently and to knock even with importunity . . . But our Lord Jesus Christ, who is a petitioner with us and a bestower of God, would surely not exhort us so emphatically to ask if he were not willing to give. Let the slothfulness of men be put to shame — he is more willing to give than we are to receive; he is more willing to show mercy than we are to be delivered from our misery, and no doubt if we are not delivered we shall remain in our misery. For the exhortation that he gives is given for our sakes. Let us wake up, then, and believe him who exhorts us and obey him who promises us and rejoice in him who gives to us . . . He will not — like that friend in the parable — arise and give you as if he were overcome by your importunity. He wants to give. But perhaps, in spite of all your knocking, you have not yet received? Then, knock on — he wants to give. But what he wants to give he defers, so that you may desire it more ardently still — if given quickly, it might be lightly esteemed."[78]

"For you remember that a person in want came to the house of his friend and begged three loaves of him. And he, it is said, being in bed, answered saying: *The door is shut now and my children and I are in bed* (Luke 11:5-8). But he, through persevering petition, extorted by importunity what he could not gain of his own deserts. But God is willing to give, only he does not give except to the one who asks, for fear he give to one who will not receive it. He does not need to be roused by your importunity. For when you pray, you are not troublesome to him as you would be to one who sleeps. *Indeed he neither slumbers nor sleeps, the guardian of Israel* (Psalm 121:4)."[79] The man who wanted three loaves of bread at midnight received them, because, says Augustine, "he did not leave off knocking, because even when his request was refused he did not turn away. He who was not willing to give, gave what was asked because the other did not 'faint' in asking. How much more shall that Good One give who exhorts us to ask, who is displeased if we do not ask?"[80]

"Have you, perhaps, prayed for something and not received it? Then have trust in a Father who would give were it expedient for you. Let me propose a case that might be your own. What your child — inexperienced in the ways of the world — is to you, such are you in the eyes of the Lord, for you know not the ways of God. Imagine your child crying before you the livelong day for the gift of some tool, such as a knife or a sword. You refuse to grant such a request; you would rather not give him a sword. You pay no heed to a weeping child for fear you have to lament a dying child. Again, the child screams, throws himself on the ground, dashes about that you may mount him on a horse. You refuse because he cannot yet manage a horse. He might be thrown and killed. You deny him a part of your goods but you are preserving all you have for him. You now deny him a part that might prove dangerous so that he may grow and safely enjoy all that you possess."[81] "In this present world with its many miseries we have no other refuge save knocking in prayer, believing and holding fast in our hearts the fixed principle that our Father does not give what is inexpedient for us. You know what you want; he knows what is good for you."[82]

The psalmist says: *The eyes of all look hopefully to you, and you give them their food in due season* (Psalm 145:15). Preaching on these words, Augustine reminds us that God's motives are hidden from us, but that he always has our good at heart when he seems to leave our prayers unanswered — sometimes even when we pray for things that should be agreeable in his eyes. "Sometimes," says Augustine, "a person is not heard when asking God for something quite fitting. Of course, if he is asking for something unfitting, he is only heard to his cost. But if he is not heard when asking for something by no means unfitting, he should not be downcast, nor should he give up prayer. He should continue to look for the food that God shall give *in due season.* When he fails to grant it, he does so lest what he gives should prove harmful. The Apostle prayed for nothing unfitting when he asked that the sting of the flesh be removed from him — that angel of Satan that buffeted him — yet, he was not heard. It was still necessary that he should exercise patience; it was not yet time for *food in due season.* So God said to him: *My grace is enough for you, for in weakness power reaches perfection* (2 Corinthians 12:7-9)."[83]

"It is no great thing to be heard according to your desire, but you should consider it very important to be heard to your advantage. Even the demons were heard according to their desire when they were permitted to enter the herd of swine (cf. Job 1:9-12). The Israelites also were heard according to their desire, and when the food was still in their mouths you know what happened to them (cf. Numbers 11:3). Do not therefore consider it a great thing to be heard according to your desire. Sometimes when God is angry he grants what you desire, and when he is merciful he refuses to do so."[84]

So, it is not always a good thing to be heard according to our desires, but it is very important that we be heard to our advantage. We know what we want, but God knows what is good for us. Do you not see that the Israelites received what their guilty lust craved after, to their own detriment? While the manna was raining down from heaven upon them they wanted flesh to eat (cf. Numbers 11:32). They disdained what they had and shamelessly asked for what they had not, as if it were not better for them to have asked, not that their unseemly desires be gratified with food that was wanting, but to have their dislike removed and so be made fit to receive the food that was there. For when evil delights us and good things do not delight us, we ought to entreat God to win us back to the love of what is good, rather than to grant us what is evil."[85]

Augustine sums up this teaching in his famous letter to the Lady Proba: "God has sometimes in anger granted the request of impatient petitioners, whereas in mercy he denied it to the Apostle. For we read what the Israelites asked and in what manner they asked and obtained their request, but while their desire was granted their impatience was severely corrected. Again, as it is written, in answer to their request he gave them a king according to their heart, but not according to his own heart (cf. Samuel 8:6-7). He also granted what the devil asked, namely, that his servant Job, who was to be proved, might be tempted. He granted also the request of unclean spirits that they might enter a great herd of swine (cf. Luke 8:32). These things are written to prevent anyone thinking too highly of himself if he has received an answer when urgently asking something it would be better for him not to receive, or to prevent him from being downcast and despairing of divine compassion toward himself if he be not heard . . . Regarding such things, therefore, 'we know not what to pray for as we ought.' Accordingly, if anything is ordained in a manner contrary to our prayer, we ought to entertain no doubt whatever that it was right that the will of God and not our will should be done, patiently bearing the disappointment and in all things giving thanks to God."[86]

## Unanswered Prayer

Saint Augustine suggests that Almighty God at times leaves prayer unanswered in order to increase our desire. "He who knows what to give and to whom to give it will give to him that seeks and open to him that knocks. And if he does not give, let no one call himself forsaken. For it may be that he delays to give something, but he leaves nobody hungry. If, indeed, he does not give at the expected time, he is not scorning, but rather testing, the seeker."[87] In considering this problem of unanswered prayer, therefore, it may help us to reflect that God himself has a very practical use for it, namely, to increase our fervor in asking him. "When he sometimes defers giving," says Augustine, "he does not refuse his gifts, but renders them more desirable. Gifts that have long been desired are more agreeably received and those obtained speedily are considered cheap."[88] The psalmist says: *Why, O Lord, do you reject me; why hide me from your face?* (Psalm 88:15). "Though the psalmist puts a question and asks for an answer," observes Augustine, "he does not intend to doubt God's wisdom or to suggest that God could have acted without reason . . . If we consider the matter closely, God's reason is manifest. For the prayers of the saints are 'rejected,' as it were, only by God's delay in conferring favors and by the trials and adversity they are permitted to suffer. But this is done so that their fervor, like fire driven back by the wind, may burn more ardently still."[89]

Whatever explanations may be offered for unanswered prayer, it will always remain a source of trial and affliction to a prayerful soul. But Augustine consoles us with the thought that the affliction of spirit caused by unanswered prayer is in itself an agreeable sacrifice to God. "Within me is the victim for my offering, within me the incense to be laid at the altar, within me the victim to win the favor of my God. For *my sacrifice, O God, is a contrite spirit* (Psalm 51:19). That I have such a sacrifice within me is clear, for listen to the words: *I sing to God, my rock: 'Why do you forget me?'* (Psalm 42:10). For in truth I labor here as if you had forgotten me, though well I know that you are but testing me, that though you may put me off, you will never fail to give me what you have promised. But even so, I cannot help but say — *why do you forget me?*"[90]

Whatever reasons may be brought forward to explain apparently unanswered prayer, one thing is certain: we must never cease to pray. But here too a problem arises: for in some texts of Scripture we are told to pray without ceasing, while in another we are advised not to talk too much! Saint Paul tells us to *never cease praying* (1 Thessalonians 5:17). Saint Luke says we should be *praying always and not losing heart* (Luke 18:1). But in the Gospel according to Saint Matthew we find these words: *In your prayer do not rattle on like the pagans. They think they will win a hearing by the sheer multiplication of words* (Matthew 6:7-8). In this text we are manifestly advised to avoid verbosity, yet we are told, "always to pray and not to faint!"

Augustine offers two solutions to this problem. One way of praying always is to cherish holy desire. "The Apostle says: *Never cease praying* (1 Thessalonians 5:17); that is, we must always yearn for God in our hearts."[91] Again, Augustine says: "It is your heart's desire that is your prayer; if your desire continues without interruption your prayer continues also. Not without meaning did the Apostle say: *Never cease praying*. Does he mean that we must kneel or prostrate ourselves or lift up our hands without ever ceasing? If this is what we mean when we say that we pray, then I think it is something we cannot do always. But there is another kind of interior prayer that never ceases and that is the desire of the heart."[92] "Wherefore, it is neither wrong nor unprofitable to spend a good deal of time in prayer, if there be leisure for it and without hindering other good and necessary work to which duty calls us; although even in the performance of such duties, as I have said, we ought to pray without ceasing by cherishing holy desire. For to spend a long time in prayer is not, as some people think, the same thing as to pray with much speaking. Loquacity is one thing; long continued warmth of desire is another."[93]

The second way of praying always is by continuous right living. "Whose tongue could endure praising God all day long?" demands Augustine. "My sermon, for example, has been a little longer than usual and you are tired of it. Who, then, could endure praising God all day long? But I am going to suggest a method which will enable you to do so if you so desire. Whatever you do, do it well, and you have praised God."[94] "Now, when we are gathered together in the church we praise God, but when we depart each to his own business it looks as if we cease to praise him. But let a man never cease from right living and he is always praising God. You cease to praise him when you turn aside justice and from all that pleases him. But if you never cease from right living, then, though your tongue be silent, your life is eloquent and the ear of God is open to your heart."[95]

Summing up, therefore, we may say that prayer should come from a loving heart, from a heart that is right with God. And since we pray God to give and to forgive, prayer will be more effectively offered by the one who is himself prepared to give and to forgive. It must be made, moreover, with a view to salvation and with greater concern for spiritual than for material gain. Finally, it is most efficaciously offered by the one who is convinced of his own mortal need, whose soul throbs with continuous pious emotion toward the Lord, and who asks with the persistence of a lover who will not be denied. These are the qualities of truly effective prayer. Man must pray, he must speak the truth when he prays, and he must pray as the Savior taught him — in the Lord's Prayer.

CHAPTER 6

# THE LORD'S PRAYER

## "Lord, Teach Us to Pray"

"IF YOU HAD A CASE IN COURT," observes Augustine, "and you wished to present a petition to the Emperor, you would consult a learned man, skilled in the law, and ask him to compose the petition for you; lest, perhaps, you approach the throne in some manner other than the approved one, and not only fail to obtain your request, but be considered worthy of censure rather than favor. When, therefore, the apostles wished to make a petition and were not sure how to approach Almighty God, they said to Christ, *Lord, teach us to pray.* That is to say: 'You, our advocate, our lawyer, our associate justice with God, you draw up our petition for us.' And from the Book of Heavenly Law, the Lord taught them — he taught them how to pray . . ."[1]

> *This is how you are to pray:*
>
> *Our Father in heaven, hallowed be your name, your kingdom come, your will be done on earth as it is in heaven. Give us today our daily bread, and forgive us the wrong we have done as we forgive those who wrong us. Subject us not to the trial but deliver us from the evil one* (Matthew 6:9-13).

We have already remarked that words are used in prayer not for the instruction of God but for the construction of our own desires. Augustine points out that they are necessary for us, "so that they may assist us in considering and observing what we ask, and not as a means whereby we expect God to be either informed or moved to compliance."[2] The words employed by our Divine Lord in his prayer, consequently, are not intended to convey information to God, but to remind us of the things we ought to be desiring and asking of him. "Faith, hope, and charity lead unto God the man who prays, that is, the man who believes, who hopes, who desires, and he is guided as to what he should ask of the Lord by studying the Lord's Prayer."[3] This is the standard and prototype of all Christian prayer of petition, and while we may employ other words and phrases, other formulas and expressions, Augustine maintains that, "if we pray rightly and as becomes our needs we can say nothing but what is already contained in this prayer of our Lord."[4] If we had need of anything else, our Savior would most certainly have expressed it in this prayer he so formally taught us. "Whoever says anything in prayer that finds no place in that Gospel prayer is praying in a manner which, if it be not unlawful, is at least not spiritual. I know not how 'carnal' prayers can be lawful, since it behooves those who are born again of the Spirit not to pray except in a spiritual manner."[5]

Augustine goes on to demonstrate how "all the words of pious prayers" may be reduced to the petitions of the Lord's Prayer. "For example," he explains, "when one prays: *Show us your glory. Thus they will know, as we know, that there is no God but you* and *let your prophets be proved true* (Sirach 36:3-4, 15), what does he say but *Hallowed be your name*? When a person says: *O Lord of hosts, restore us; if your face shine upon us, then we shall be safe* (Psalm 80:8), what is he saying but *Your kingdom come*? When one says: *Steady my footsteps according to your promise, and let no iniquity rule over me* (Psalm 119:133), what else is he saying but *Your will be done on earth as it is in heaven*? When a person says: *Give me neither poverty nor riches* (Proverbs 30:8), what does he say but *Give us today our daily bread*? When he says: *Remember, O Lord, for David all his anxious care* (Psalm 132:1), or *O Lord, my God, if I am at fault in this, if there is guilt on my hands, if I repaid my friends with evil* (Psalm 7:4-5), what is this but *Forgive us the wrong we have done as we forgive those who wrong us*? And when he says: *Ward off passion from my heart, let not the lustful cravings of the flesh master me, surrender me not to shameless desires* (Sirach 23:5-6), what does he say but *Subject us not to the trial*? Finally, when a person says: *Rescue me from my enemies, O my God; from my adversaries defend me* (Psalm 59:2), what is this but *Deliver us from the evil one*? And so, if you go over all the words of pious prayers, you will, I believe, find nothing which cannot be contained and summed up in the Lord's Prayer. Wherefore, when we pray we are free to use different words to any extent, but we must ask the same things. In this we have no choice."[6]

In this prayer we find the expression of all our legitimate desires before the Lord. "The words employed by our Lord Jesus Christ in his prayer constitute the form for the expression of our desires. It is not lawful to pray for anything but what is here inscribed."[7] "For many ask for what they should not ask. Therefore, he who prays must beware of two things: that he does not ask for what he ought not to ask, and that he ask not from one whom he ought not to ask. From the devil, from idols, from evil spirits, must nothing be asked. From the Lord our God Jesus Christ, from God the Father of prophets and martyrs, from the Father of our Lord Jesus Christ, from God who made heaven and earth, the sea and all things in them — from him must we ask whatever we ask. But we must beware of asking for what we should not ask."[8]

If there be anything we desire from God, therefore, that is not contained in this prayer, we are asking for something we should not desire. "He who says in prayer: 'O Lord, multiply my riches,' or 'Increase my honors; make me eminent for power and fame in this world,' or something else of that kind . . . I do not think he will find any part of the Lord's Prayer into which he could fit such requests. We should at least be ashamed to ask for such things, if we are not ashamed of desiring them. If, however, we are ashamed even of desiring them but feel ourselves overcome by temptation, how much better it would be to ask that we be liberated from the plague of such desires by him to whom we say: *Deliver us from the evil one.*"[9]

It would be very difficult, then, to overestimate the importance of understanding this sublime prayer and of realizing the exact meaning of its petitions. Only by so doing shall we make ourselves aware of the things we should desire from God and the right order of their desiring. For "we have received a rule of prayer from the Lord, and it must not be transgressed either by adding or omitting anything."[10] Let us follow Augustine as he analyzes each of its petitions for us.

## Our Father Who Are in Heaven

"Seeing that when we pray we must first of all endeavor to win the goodwill of him whom we address, and then state our petition, we should seek that goodwill by praising him. This is generally done at the beginning of the prayer. In this case our Divine Lord bids us to say simply: *Our Father in heaven.*"[11] By this mode of address we rouse our affections — for a father is always dear to his children — and we assume also that suppliant disposition so necessary in prayer. Moreover, by calling God our Father we increase our confidence, "since before we ask for anything we have already received the great privilege of addressing God as our Father. What would he refuse his children having already given in advance this great gift, that they should be his sons? And what a responsibility rests upon the soul, of taking care that it be not unworthy of such a Father!"[12]

"Remember that you were born of your father Adam unto death, but you are to be born again of God the Father unto life (Augustine was speaking to Catechumens). And what you say, say in your hearts. If only you have the earnest affection of prayer, you will enjoy the effective answer of him who hears your prayer."[13] But even though, on our Divine Lord's exhortation, we address God as our Father, nevertheless, we should not forget to approach him with gratitude and with humility, realizing our unworthiness. For, in calling God our Father we claim a relationship to which we have no strict right; a relationship moreover, which we could not purchase at any price, which we enjoy only through his gratuitous benevolence. "He is God, and he is a father; God in power, a father in goodness. How fortunate you are to have found a father in your Lord: Have faith in him, and promise yourself all things from his mercy because he is almighty."[14]

In Old Testament times it was only the chosen people who called upon God in prayer, but the prophet Joel foretold that a time would come when all men would call upon God. *Then everyone shall be rescued who calls on the name of the Lord* (Joel 3:5). Saint Paul, the Apostle of the Gentiles, quoted this prophecy in his epistle to the Romans (Romans 10:13). When we say the "Our Father," therefore, we acknowledge that we are the brothers of

Christ and that all men are brethren. "And here an admonition is given to the rich and to those whom the world considers well-born, that when they become Christians they are not to lord it over the poor and the lowly, seeing that together with them they address God as 'Our Father' — an expression they cannot use with truth and piety unless they recognize the poor as their brethren."[15]

"The inheritance which he promises us is such that many may possess it and no one be short; therefore has he called unto his brotherhood the peoples of the nations, so that the only Son has numberless brethren who say: *Our Father who are in heaven.* So said they who have gone before us; so shall they say who will come after us. See how many brethren the only Son has in his grace, sharing his inheritance with those for whom he suffered death! We had a father and mother on earth that we might be born to labor and death, but we have found other parents: God our Father, and the Church our Mother, by whom we are born unto life eternal. Let us, then, consider whose children we have begun to be, and let us live as becomes those who have such a father."[16]

Now, this Father of ours is in heaven; consequently, we are advised to seek him there. "Cling not, therefore, to the things of the earth, for you have found a father in heaven. You have been affiliated to a new race. Under this father, the master and the slave are brethren; the rich and the poor are brethren; the commander-in-chief and the common soldier are brethren. Faithful Christians all have different fathers on earth, some of high degree, others of lowly origin, but they all invoke the One Father who is in heaven. If our Father is in heaven, then, an inheritance is provided for us there. But he is such a father that we can still have him together with what he gives. For though he gives an inheritance it is not by dying that he leaves it to us. He never dies; he lives forever that we may come to him. Since, then, you know of whom you ask, know also what to ask, for fear you offend such a father by asking amiss."[17] "We have found, then, a father in heaven; let us take good heed how we live on earth. For he who has found such a father ought so to live that he may come into his inheritance."[18]

## Hallowed Be Your Name

"And now, having stated who he is to whom we pray, let us consider what we are to pray for. The first petition of all is: *Hallowed be your name.* This petition is not to be understood as if God's name were not already holy, but one expresses the desire that God's name may be considered holy by all men. That is, that God may be so well known to men that they will consider nothing more holy than his name and dread nothing more than to offend it. It has been said: *God, renowned in Judah, in Israel great is his name* (Psalm 76:2), not as if his name were less known in one place than in another, but the name of God is great where it is uttered with due deference to his majesty. So, his name is called holy where it is used with reverence and with the fear of offending him."[19]

"What is the meaning of 'to be hallowed'? It means, 'to be considered holy'; to be not despised."[20] But why should we pray that God's name may be accounted holy? His name IS holy. "But when you pray that his name may be hallowed, you are not, as it appears, praying to him for his sake and not for your own. No. Understand this petition properly and you will see that it is for yourself that you pray. For this is what you ask, namely, that what is always holy in itself may be hallowed in you . . . You see, therefore, that the good you desire is for yourself. For if you despise the name of God it will be bad for you, not for him."[21]

In making this petition, therefore, we do not pray for God, but for ourselves. God's name is always holy, but we pray that by the invocation of his name in baptism, we may be rendered holy. "How is his name hallowed in us," demands Augustine, "except insofar as it makes us holy? For once we were not holy, and we are made holy by his name (in baptism). But he is always holy and his name is always holy. So, it is for ourselves and not for God that we pray. We do not wish well to God to whom no evil can ever happen. But we desire what is good for ourselves, that his holy name may be hallowed in us, that that which is always holy may be hallowed in us."[22] "This hallowing of God's name is that whereby we are made holy."[23] "The name of God is hallowed in you when you are baptized. Why will you offer this prayer after you have been baptized, except it be for this reason, that that which you shall then receive may abide in you forever?"[24]

Moreover, in saying this petition of the Lord's Prayer, we do not pray merely for ourselves, but for others also — even for those who are not of the faith. "You pray, furthermore," says Augustine, "that the name of God be considered holy by those who through unbelief do not hold it in reverence . . . You pray for the human race, you pray for the whole world, for all those who daily sit in judgment on God and argue that he is not just. You pray that they may be corrected and may reform their hearts to the image of his righteousness, that they may no longer insult him . . . *How good God is to the upright; the Lord, to those who are clean of heart!* (Psalm 73:1)."[25]

The proud of this world do not desire that God's name be hallowed. *They certainly had knowledge of God, yet they did not glorify him as God or give him thanks* (Romans 1:21). "They wish rather that their own name be celebrated, and they do not praise the name of the Lord. Therefore, *they stultified themselves through speculating to no purpose, and their senseless hearts were darkened. They claimed to be wise, but turned into fools instead* (Romans 1:21-22). They wish their own name to be celebrated far and wide, they who are soon to pass into the grave. It becomes God, it becomes the Lord, to be both always and everywhere proclaimed. *Blessed be the name of the Lord both now and forever* (Psalm 113:2). "Let him be proclaimed everywhere: *From the rising to the setting of the sun is the name of the Lord to be praised* (Psalm 113:3).

## Your Kingdom Come

Here, again, Augustine points out that we must not imagine that when we say these words we are praying for God, as though he had not ruled all creation since the world began. He suggests that this petition is a prayer that the kingdom of God be made manifest to all men, and that we ourselves may be worthy citizens of it some day. "Just as light that is present is, nevertheless, absent to those who are blind or to those who shut their eyes, so also is the kingdom of God, though it never departs from the earth, absent to those who know nothing of it."[26] We pray, therefore, that the knowledge and love of this kingdom may come to all men. We pray, furthermore, for ourselves that we may one day be members of God's kingdom.

"The kingdom of God shall come whether you ask for it or not. Why, then, do you make this petition, unless it be that what is coming for all the saints may come also for you — that God will include you in the number of his elect to whom his kingdom shall come?"[27] "But what kingdom do you wish for? That of which it is written in the Gospel: *Come. You have my Father's blessing! Inherit the kingdom prepared for you from the creation of the world* (Matthew 25:34). Behold, here is the kingdom of which you say, *Your kingdom come.* You desire that it may come to you, that you may be a member of it. For come it certainly shall, but what will it profit you if its advent finds you at the left hand? Therefore, here again it is to yourself that you wish well, for yourself that you pray. You hope that you may so live, that one day you may belong to the kingdom of God, which is the reward of all the saints. Therefore, when you say, *Your kingdom come,* you pray for yourself, that you may live a holy life. May we, O Lord, belong to your kingdom; may we enjoy one day what has already come to the saints!"[28]

"Come it certainly shall whether we ask for it or not. Indeed, God has an eternal kingdom. When did he not reign? When did he begin to reign? His kingdom has no beginning, neither shall it have any end. But that you may know that in this petition also we pray for ourselves and not for God — for we do not say, *Your kingdom come* as if we were asking that God might reign — we ourselves shall be his kingdom if, believing in him, we make progress in this faith. All the faithful redeemed by the blood of his only Son will be his kingdom. And this kingdom shall come when the resurrection of the dead shall have taken place. Then he will come himself, and when the dead are risen he will divide them, as he himself says, *Then he will separate them into two groups, as a shepherd separates sheep from goats. The sheep he will place on his right hand, the goats on his left* (Matthew 25:32-33). To those on his right hand he will say, *Come. You have my Father's blessing!*

*Inherit the kingdom* (Matthew 25:34). This is what we desire and pray for when we say, *Your kingdom come;* that it may come to us. But if we be reckoned with the reprobates, the kingdom will come to others but not to us."[29]

"We yearn for his kingdom to come, and come it shall, even should we wish that it would not. But to wish and to pray that his kingdom may come is nothing other than desiring that he would make us worthy of his kingdom, lest perhaps — which God forbid — it should come, but not to us. For to many that kingdom will never come, even though it must come. It will come to those to whom it shall be said, *Come. You have my Father's blessing! Inherit the kingdom prepared for you from the creation of the world.* But it will not come to those to whom it shall be said, *Out of my sight, you condemned, into that everlasting fire* (Matthew 25:41). Therefore, when we say, *Your kingdom come,* we pray that it may come to us. What is the meaning of 'may come to us'? It means that the coming of God's kingdom may find us good. We pray for this, therefore, that he may make us good, for then shall his kingdom come to us."[30]

## Your Will Be Done on Earth as It Is in Heaven

In this petition also it is for ourselves and not for God that we pray. Certainly the will of God will be done both in heaven and on earth whether we like it or not, whether we pray for it or not. Augustine charges his catechumens, saying: "Remember what you have repeatedly said in the Creed, 'I believe in God the Father Almighty.' If he be almighty why do you pray that his will may be done? Then, what is the meaning of this petition: *Your will be done*? It means 'May it be done in me, so that I do not resist your will.' For the will of God shall be done *in* you, even though it may not be done *by* you. For both in those to whom he shall say, *Come. You have my Father's blessing! Inherit the kingdom prepared for you from the creation of the world* (Matthew 25:34), shall the will of God be done, that the saints and the just may receive the kingdom; and in those to whom he shall say, *Out of my sight, you condemned, into that everlasting fire prepared for the devil and his angels* (Matthew 25:41) shall his will be done, that the wicked may be condemned to everlasting fire. That his will may be done *by* you is another thing. It is not, then, without reason that you pray that his will may be done in you in such a manner that it may be good for you. For whether it be good or bad for you, it shall still be done *in* you. But, oh, that it may be done *by* you!"[31]

Augustine offers many interpretations of this petition dependent upon the many ways in which one may interpret the terms, "heaven" and "earth." In the following passage from one of his sermons, he shows the wealth of meaning that may be read into these simple words: *Your will be done on earth as it is in heaven.* "In the Church, the spiritual are heaven, and the carnal are the earth. So, then, *Your will be done on earth as it is in heaven* means that as those who are spiritual serve you, so let those who are carnal be reformed and serve you also . . . And there is still another very spiritual meaning for this petition. For we are admonished to pray for our enemies. The Church is heaven, the enemies of the Church are the earth. What, then, is the meaning of *Your will be done on earth as it is in heaven*? May our enemies believe in you as we also believe in you! May they become friends and cease to be enemies. They are the earth and for that reason are they against us; may they become heavenly and so be one with us."[32]

Augustine maintains that heaven and earth may be understood as saint and sinner. To the first sinner God Almighty said: "Earth you are and to earth you shall return"; whereas of the saints it is said: "For the temple of God is holy which you are." "There is as much difference spiritually between a saint and a sinner, as there is materially between heaven and earth."[33] So, he offers this interpretation of the third petition. "As all the patriarchs, all the apostles, and all other saintly souls are like heaven in relation to God, while you in comparison to them are like the earth — *Your will be done on earth as it is in heaven* — so may God's will be done in you as it is in them."[34]

This petition will be fully and securely realized only "when death shall be swallowed up in victory and this corruptible has put on incorruption." In other words, in the next life. "This shall be the essence of supreme peace in life eternal, not only to desire what is good, but to be able to do it. *The desire to do right is there but not the power* (Romans 7:18). The reason being that the will of God is not yet done on earth as it is in heaven, is not yet done in the flesh as in the spirit."[35]

"Now, all these things which we have mentioned, these three petitions, my beloved, have reference to life eternal. For if the name of God is sanctified in us, it will be for eternity. If his kingdom come in which we shall live forever, it will be for eternity. If his will be done as in heaven so on earth, in all the ways I have explained, it will be so for eternity. "There remain now the petitions for this life of our pilgrimage; therefore, the prayer continues: *Give us today our daily bread.* That is, give us eternal things, give us things temporal. You have promised a kingdom; deny us not the means of sustenance. You will give everlasting glory with yourself hereafter; give us temporal support now, on this earth."[36]

## Give Us Today Our Daily Bread

Augustine offers three interpretations of this fourth petition, dependent on how we understand the words "daily bread." He says that we may interpret them as meaning all that is necessary to sustain our bodily health in this world, or as having reference to the sacrament of the Eucharist, or finally, as the food of our minds, that is, the word of God. He himself is inclined to favor the last of these as the best interpretation, namely, that they refer to the spiritual nourishment of God's word, though he allows that all three may be taken together. "If, however, a person chooses to take this sentence as referring to food necessary for the body, or to the sacrament of the Lord's body, then, all three may be taken together. That is to say, in the same breath we may ask for the bread that is necessary for the body, for the consecrated visible bread of the sacrament, and for the invisible bread of the word of God."[37]

This is the only petition of the Lord's Prayer in which we ask God simply and straightforwardly to "give us" something. "Now, here," says Augustine, "it is manifest that we pray for ourselves. When you say *Hallowed be your name,* it is necessary to explain that you pray for yourself and not for God. When you say *Your will be done,* this too has to be explained, for fear you think that you are wishing well to God by praying that his will may be done, whereas, in reality, you are praying for yourself. And when you say, *Your kingdom come,* this also must be explained, for fear you think that you are doing a service to God by praying that he may reign. But from here to the end of prayer it is quite clear that you pray for yourself."[38]

"It may be understood that we make this petition for daily sustenance, so that we may have plenty, or, if not that, that we may want for nothing."[39] Yet, though Augustine says that this is a good interpretation of the fourth petition, he by no means considers it to be the only one. He points out, in fact, that our Divine Lord must have intended much more than mere bodily nourishment because he himself said: *I warn you, then: Do not worry about your livelihood, what you are to eat or drink or use for clothing. Seek first his kingship over you, his way of holiness, and all these things will be given you besides* (Matthew 6:33). From which texts it would appear that our Redeemer expected us to ask for something more than a mere temporal good of the body. Our heavenly Father is accustomed to give daily bread to inferior creatures and even to those who offend him.

"But this bread, dearly beloved, by which our bodies are fed, by which the flesh is refreshed each day, this bread, I say, God gives not only to those who praise him, but to those also who blaspheme him: *This will prove that you are sons of your heavenly Father, for his sun rises on the bad and the good, he rains on the just and the unjust* (Matthew 5:45). You praise him and he feeds you; you blaspheme him and he feeds you . . . Since, then, both good and bad receive this bread from God, do you think there is no other bread from God, bread for which the children ask, and concerning which the Lord said in the Gospel, *It is not right to take the food of sons and daughters and throw it to the dogs* (Matthew 15:26)? Yes, surely there is. What, then, is that bread? And why is it called 'daily'? Because this bread is as necessary as the other, for without it we cannot live; without bread we cannot live. It is shameful to ask God for wealth, but there is no shame in asking for daily bread. That which ministers to pride is one thing, that which ministers to life is another. Nevertheless, because this bread which may be seen and handled is given both to the good and to the bad, there is a daily bread for which the children pray, and this bread is the word of God which is dealt out to us day by day."[40]

"The word of God which is explained to us and is, in a sense, broken day by day is 'daily bread.' And as our bodies hunger after that other bread, so do our souls hunger after this bread. We ask, therefore, for this bread because whatever is needful in this life both for our souls and bodies is included in the words 'daily bread'."[41] "The word I am speaking before you now is daily bread, and the lessons you hear and repeat are 'daily bread.' For all these are necessary in our state of pilgrimage. But when we shall have entered heaven, shall we then hear the word of God, we who shall see and hear the Word himself, and eat and drink him as the angels do now? Do the angels need books and interpreters and readers? Surely not. They read in seeing, for they see truth itself, and they are fully satisfied with that fountain from which we receive but a few drops. So has it been said that this petition regarding our daily bread is necessary for us only in this life."[42]

Concerning the interpretation that would consider "daily bread" as having reference to the Blessed Sacrament, Augustine says: "Again, this is a very good sense of *Give us today our daily bread,* that is, the Eucharist, our daily food. For the faithful know what they receive, and it is good for them to receive that bread which is necessary for this present time."[43] It is obvious, however, that this interpretation cannot be the only one. If it were, then the Lord's Prayer would be said once only and that before communion. "Who is there," demands Augustine, "who would venture to say that we ought to say the Lord's Prayer once only, or that we may say it a second or third time, but only up to the hour when we receive the Body of the Lord, and that afterwards we must not repeat the prayer during the rest of the day?"[44] It is clear, then, that though Augustine suggests three interpretations of this petition, all of which we may take together, he himself favored that understanding of it according to which the words "daily bread" refer to the word of God, or to the invisible and imperishable food of

God's precepts. But no matter what interpretation we choose, or whether we choose all three, it is manifest that this fourth petition concerns this life and not life eternal.

"But when this life shall have ended, we shall seek neither that bread which hunger seeks, nor shall we have to receive the sacrament of the altar, because we shall be there with Christ whose body we now receive. Neither shall these words we are now speaking be needful for you nor the sacred volume read. For we shall see him who is himself the Word of God, by whom all things were made, by whom the angels are fed, by whom the angels are enlightened, by whom the angels become wise, not needing words of circuitous discourse, but drinking in the only Word, filled with whom they burst forth in neverending praise. *Happy they,* says the psalmist, *who dwell in your house! Continually they praise you* (Psalm 84:5)."[45]

## Forgive Us the Wrong We Have Done As We Forgive Those Who Wrong Us

"When you offer your petitions to God, examine your hearts and see whether you do not pass over the petition, *Forgive us the wrong we have done as we forgive those who wrong us.* For you will not really be praying unless you make that petition. If you substitute something else for it, he may not hear you, for your devices were not dictated by the lawgiver sent from God. Consequently, even when we use our own words in prayer, we must pray according to the norm he has given us."[46]

The term "the wrong" in this fifth petition means in the first place, the sins that we ourselves commit against God, and in the second place, the sins committed against us by our neighbors. "Here, then, it is not financial indebtedness as such that one is urged to remit, but to forgive whatever offense another has committed against him."[47] The words are not used, therefore, merely in reference to money, but to all the ways in which anyone may offend us. They may also refer, of course, to a financial debt. "For the man who refuses to pay you the money he owes you when he has the means to do so sins against you. And if you do not forgive this sin, you will not be able to say, *Forgive us as we forgive.*[48] "It is impossible for one to say truthfully that he is praying for someone whom he refuses to forgive."[49] "Regarding this petition, once again we need no explanation that it is for ourselves that we pray. For we beg that our debts may be forgiven us. Debtors indeed we are, not in money, but in sins. You are saying to yourselves, perhaps, at this moment: 'What about you?' We answer, yes, we too. What, you holy bishops! Are you debtors? Yes, we too are debtors. What, you! My Lord, be it far from you to do yourself this wrong. I do myself no wrong, but I speak the truth; we are debtors: *If we say, 'We are free of the guilt of sin,' we deceive ourselves; the truth is not to be found in us* (1 John 1:8)."[50]

Exhorting his catechumens, Augustine said: "Let us say everyday, and say in sincerity of heart, and let us *do* what we say: *Forgive us the wrong we have done as we forgive those who wrong us.* It is an engagement, a covenant, an agreement we make with God. The Lord your God says to you: 'Forgive and I will forgive. You have not forgiven? Then, you retain your own sins against yourself, not I.' I pray you, then, my dearly beloved children, since I know what is expedient for you in the Lord's Prayer, and particularly in that sentence of it, *Forgive us the wrong we have done as we forgive those who wrong us,* I pray you, hear me. You are about to be baptized; forgive everything; whatever any man has in his heart against any other, let him from his heart forgive it."[51]

Though Augustine admits that it is not easy to forgive those who have injured us, nevertheless, he insists that we must strive after this perfection. God commands it, and he would not command the impossible. By his grace only can it be done. "You have enemies," he says, "for who could live on this earth without them? Take heed to yourself and love them. In no way can the violence of your enemy so hurt you, as you can hurt yourself if you do not love him. He may injure your estate, your flocks, or your home; he may injure your man-servant or your maid-servant, your son or your wife; or, at most, if such power be given him, he can injure you physically. But can he injure your soul as you can injure it yourself? Reach forward to this power, dearly beloved. Only he can give it to whom you say: *Your will be done on earth as it is in heaven.* Do not let it appear impossible to you. I know, I know from experience that there are Christians who love their enemies. If it seems impossible to you, you will not do it. Believe, first of all, that it can be done, and then pray that the will of God may be done in you."[52]

Our holy Mother the Church gives us a very good example in this respect, for she prayed for her persecutor Saul and gained his conversion. "For Saul was an enemy of the Church; prayer was made for him, and he became her friend. He not only ceased to persecute her, he labored to help her. And yet, to tell the truth, the prayer was made against him, that is, against his malice, not against his nature as a person. So let your prayer be against the malice of your enemy that it may die, but that he may live. If your enemy were dead, it might be that you had lost an enemy, but you certainly would not have found a friend. But should his malice die, at one and the same time you will have lost an enemy and found a friend."[53]

There are those who think that it is too much to expect of man, that he should forgive those who have injured him. Augustine realized this only too well, for on one occasion he said: "May God bring it to effect in your hearts! I know as well as you that there are few who do it; great men and spiritual men are they who do it. Are all the faithful in the Church who approach the altar and receive the body and blood of Christ, are they all such? Yet, they all say, *Forgive us the wrong we have done as we forgive those who wrong us.* How can you do this if you do not love your enemies? What then must we do, brethren? Is the flock of Christ reduced to such a scanty few? If those only ought to say, *Forgive us the wrong we have done as we forgive those who wrong us,* who love their enemies, then I do not know what to do, I do not know what to say. Must I say to you that if you do not love your enemies, then do not pray! I dare not say that: rather should I say, pray that you may be able to love them. Or must I say, that if you do not love your enemies, then do not say in the Lord's Prayer, *Forgive us the wrong we have done as we forgive those who wrong us*? Suppose I were to say, 'Do not use these words!' If you do not, your debts are not forgiven, and if you do use them and do not act accordingly, your debts are not forgiven. In order, therefore, that you may be forgiven, you must not only use the words, you must do what you say."[54]

A distinction is made in this matter which may console those who find it hard to forgive. It is certainly a lot to ask that we forgive a person who is presently and actively violent against us. We may not as yet be sufficiently advanced in virtue to follow the example of our Divine Lord on the cross. Nevertheless, Augustine insists that if an enemy comes to us and asks our pardon, then we must forgive. If we refuse forgiveness in these circumstances, the results to our own souls will be disastrous. "If the Lord be too high an example for you, turn your thoughts to your fellow servant, Saint Stephen. He was being stoned by his enemies, and as they stoned him, he prayed for them on bended knees, saying, *Lord, do not hold this sin against them* (Acts 7:60). They were casting stones, not asking pardon, yet he prayed for them. I wish you were like him; reach forward. Why are you forever trailing your hearts on the earth? Hear me, lift up your hearts, reach forward, love your enemy. If you cannot love him in his violence, love him at least when he asks your pardon. Love the man who says, 'Brother, I have offended you, forgive me.' If under these circumstances you do not forgive, I do not say merely that you blot this prayer out of your heart, but you yourself will be blotted out of the Book of Life."[55]

"The time for prayer will come, the time for you to say, *Forgive us the wrong we have done as we forgive those who wrong us*; and the Lord will answer you, *You wretched wretch! I cancelled your entire debt when you pleaded with me. Should you not have dealt mercifully with your fellow servant, as I dealt with you?* (Matthew 18:32-33). These words are out of the Gospel, not out of my own heart. But if you forgive him who asks your pardon, then, you can say this prayer. And if you have not yet the strength to love him in his violence, you may still offer this prayer, *Forgive us the wrong we have done as we forgive those who wrong us.*"[56] However, as we have already remarked, in this latter case, we must pray God that we may be able to love them. "You, brethren, who, taking advantage of this occasion, are listening to this prayer and to our exposition of it, do you wholly and from your hearts forgive whatever you have against any person. Forgive it there where God sees it. Sometimes a man remits with his mouth and retains the offense in his heart — he remits with his lips for the sake of men and retains in his heart not fearing the eyes of God. But do you remit entirely? Whatever you have retained up to these holy days, in these holy days at least, remit. *The sun must not go down on your wrath* (Ephesians 4:26) — but many suns have set!"[57]

There are two passions in man which make the forgiving of those who injure us very difficult indeed, and these are the closely related passions of anger and hatred. In the following very interesting passage Augustine defines them and explains how one grows out of the other. "What, then, is anger? The lust of vengeance. And what is hatred? Inveterate anger . . . What was anger when it was born became hatred because it had grown old. Anger is a mote, hatred is a beam. We sometimes find fault with one who is angry, yet we retain hatred in our own hearts. So Christ said to us: *Why look at the speck in your brother's eye when you miss the plank in your own?* (Matthew 7:3). How did the speck grow into a plank? Because it was not plucked out at once. Because you allowed the sun to rise and set so often upon your anger, you made it inveterate. Because you entertained evil suspicions you watered the speck; by watering it you nourished it; by nourishing it you made it a plank. Tremble, then, at least when it is said, *Anyone who hates his brother is a murderer* (1 John 3:15)."[58]

"Accordingly, my brethren, I enjoin you, who are my sons in the grace of God . . . I enjoin you, that when anyone offends or sins against you and confesses and asks your pardon, you pardon him at once, and from your heart forgive him, for fear you keep from yourselves the pardon that comes from God. For if you forgive not, neither shall he forgive you."[59]

## Subject Us Not to the Trial

"So much have we said regarding past sins: What now of the future?"[60] "The sixth petition is: *Subject us not to the trial.* A number of codices have 'lead,' which is, I think, equivalent in meaning, for both are equivalents of the Greek word Εισενεγκῃς. When praying, many people say: 'Do not permit us to be led into temptation,' evidently essaying an explanation of how the word 'lead' is used. God himself does not, of course, lead us into temptation, but by a most hidden economy and because one deserves it, he permits him whom he has left without his aid to be so led . . . But to be led into temptation is one thing, to be tempted is another. For without a trial no one can win approval, not even self-approval; as it is written: *One never put to the proof knows little* (Sirach 34:10).[61]

The only kind of temptation, then, into which God leads a soul is temptation in the sense of a test or trial of virtue. *For the Lord, your God, is testing you to know whether you really love him with all your heart and with all your soul* (Deuteronomy 13:4). In this text, the words "to know," really mean, "to make you know," whether you love him. For to God, "who knows all things before they come to pass, we are known even before any temptation occurs."[62] Again, in the Gospel according to Saint John, we read of the feeding of the five thousand, before which Christ had asked the Apostle Philip: *Where shall we buy bread for these people to eat?* (John 6:5). And the Gospel continues, saying, *He knew well what he intended to do but he asked this to test Philip's response* (John 6:6). Commenting on these words, Augustine says: "Now, if he knew the heart of him whom he was putting on trial, what is there that he wished to know by testing him? Surely it was done, so that he who was being tried might learn to know himself and condemn his own lack of confidence, when he saw the hunger of the crowds appeased by the bread of the Lord, while he had thought that they had nothing to eat?"[63]

Augustine points out that this petition has reference only to this life, as it is only in this life that souls are subject to temptation. "We read in the book of holy Job, *Is not man's life on earth a drudgery?* (Job 7:1). What, then, do we pray for? Hear what the Apostle Saint James says: *No one who is tempted is free to say, 'I am being tempted by God'* (James 1:13). He spoke of those evil temptations whereby men are deceived and brought under the yoke of the devil. This is the kind of temptation called a testing: of this kind of temptation it is written: *For the Lord, your God, is testing you to know whether you really love him* (Deuteronomy 13:4). What is the meaning of 'to know'? It means, 'to make you know,' for he himself knows already. With that kind of temptation, however, whereby we are deceived and seduced, God tempts no man. But, undoubtedly, in his deep and hidden judgment, he abandons some: and when he has abandoned them, the tempter finds his opportunity. For the devil finds no resistance in one so abandoned: if God abandons a soul, the tempter immediately enters as that soul's possessor. Therefore, that God may not abandon us in this way, we say: *Subject us not to the trial.*"[64]

To be led into temptation means to be subjected to temptations under which we would fall. "We are led into them if they are such that we cannot endure."[65] Augustine observes, furthermore, that there is a difference in the temptations under which a man may fall. "For example, Judas, who sold his Master, did not fall into a temptation of the same nature as that of Peter, when, under the influence of terror, he denied his Lord. There are, I believe, temptations that are human, as when, for instance, a person fails to live up to a resolution through human frailty, or becomes irritated with a brother who in his zeal to correct him goes beyond the bounds of Christian moderation. Concerning such temptations the Apostle says: *No test has been sent you that does not come to all men* (1 Corinthians 10:13), and he also says, *He will not let you be tested beyond your strength. Along with the test he will give you a way out of it so that you may be able to endure it* (1 Corinthians 10:13). In that sentence he makes it quite clear that we are not to pray that we may not be tempted, but that we may not be led into temptation."[66]

## But Deliver Us From Evil

"The seventh and last petition is, *Deliver us from evil.* For we must pray, not only not to be led into temptation from which we are as yet free (that request was made in the sixth petition) but also, that we may be delivered from evil into which we have already fallen."[67] Now, there is one thing that can prevent our being delivered from the evil of sin already committed, and that is a refusal on our part to forgive those who have sinned against us. If we have lost the faculty of forgiving those who have injured us, our own sins will not be forgiven before God, and our prayer, *Deliver us from evil,* will be sadly ineffective. At this point, therefore, Augustine reverts to the fifth petition, emphasizing its importance as a necessary condition for the effectiveness of the seventh. Consequently, the temptation we must seek to avoid above all others is the temptation to anger, which is a craving for vengeance. "If you have committed sins other than anger, such as sins of the senses or sins of lust, you may be cured insofar as you are still able to say, *Forgive us the wrong we have done as we forgive those who wrong us.* When that power is lost, all your sins are retained, nothing at all is remitted."[68] We cannot appeal with any hope of success to the mercy of God, saying, *Deliver us from evil,* if we ourselves refuse mercy to others.

Let us mark this well. When our Divine Lord composed this prayer, he continued on after the words, *Deliver us from evil,* were spoken, and he immediately added: *If you forgive the faults of others, your heavenly Father will forgive you yours. If you do not forgive others, neither will your Father forgive you* (Matthew 6:14-15). In other words, the seventh petition will be effective, only on condition that we *do* what we say in the fifth. And we say there, *Forgive us the wrong we have done as we forgive those who wrong us*. Augustine draws our attention to this, saying: "Our Lord, our Master and Savior, knowing the danger of this temptation (to anger) in this life, when he taught us the seven petitions of this prayer, took none of them to comment on himself or to recommend with greater emphasis than this one . . . Passing over all the others, he taught us this one with a remarkable insistence. There was no need to insist so much on those sins, in which if a man offends, he may know how to be cured; but there was need of it with reference to that sin, into which if a man falls, there is no means whereby the rest may be cured. For this reason you ought to be forever saying, *Forgive us the wrong we have done . . . Forgive us the wrong we have done as we forgive those who wrong us.* If you have lost this faculty, you are lost yourself."[69] We shall not be delivered from the evil of sin committed, except on condition that we forgive those who trespass against us.

"Take heed, my brethren, my sons, sons of God, take heed, I beseech you, to what I am saying. Fight to the limit of your powers against your own hearts. If you see your anger making a stand against you, pray God to make you conqueror over yourself. Pray that he may help you to conquer not, I say, your enemy outside, but your own soul within. He will help you, and you shall find that you are able to do it."[70] If we can conquer the inclination to seek vengeance and so preserve the faculty of forgiving those who have injured us, then, our heavenly Father will forgive us our offenses, and the prayer, *Deliver us from evil,* shall be answered. Good must be done, evil must be avoided: this is the basis of all morality. To keep this principle before our minds and to put it into practice in our daily lives is great wisdom and should be our constant prayer. "The wisdom that is granted even in this life," declares Augustine, "is not to be despised by faithful servants of God. And that wisdom is that we avoid with the greatest vigilance what, from the Lord's revelation, we know must be avoided, and that we pursue with the utmost devotion what that same revelation incites us to seek after. By so doing, when death relieves us of our mortality in our appointed time, the happiness of the whole man will be secured — a happiness which begins in this life and which we now strain every effort to attain in its fullness some day."[71]

This prayer constitutes the formula for the expression of all a Christian's legitimate, prayerful desires before the Lord. "When, therefore, we say: *Hallowed be your name,* we admonish ourselves to desire that his name, which is always holy, may be esteemed as holy, that is, not despised, among men; which is an advantage, not to God, but to all men. When we say: *Your kingdom come* — as come it certainly shall, whether we wish it or not — we stir up our own desires for that kingdom by means of these words; we desire that it may come to us, that we may be found worthy to reign in it. When we say: *Your will be done on earth as it is in heaven,* we pray for ourselves that he may give us the grace of obedience, so that his will may be done by us as it is done in heavenly places by his angels. When we say: *Give us today our daily bread,* the word 'today' signifies for the present time, in which we ask for that competency of temporal blessings which I have spoken of before . . . or the sacrament of believers which is necessary in this present time; not however to obtain temporal, but rather eternal felicity. When we say: *Forgive us the wrong we have done as we forgive those who wrong us,* we remind ourselves both what we should ask and what we should do in order to be worthy of receiving what we ask. When we say: *Subject us not to the trial,* we admonish ourselves to desire that we may not, through being deprived of God's help, be either ensnared to consent or incited to yield to temptation. When we say: *Deliver us from evil,* we admonish ourselves to consider that we do not yet enjoy that good estate in which we shall experience no evil . . . It was necessary that by the use of these words the things they signify should be kept before our memory."[72]

"These things it is our duty to ask, and without hesitation, both for ourselves and for our friends, for strangers also, yes, even for our enemies . . ."[73] The plural form in which this prayer of our Lord is expressed suggests not only the consciousness of association with others when we pray, but the desire also that all others should share the gifts of God together with us. This prayer is the perfect expression of a Christian's love, and that love is but the prolongation on earth of Christ's love for man. Beyond doubt, that love was made manifest in his desire to have sharers in his inheritance. That is why he "has called into his brotherhood the peoples of the nations, so that the only Son has numberless brethren who say: *Our Father in heaven.*"[74] As the attribute of community is essential to Christian love, it is likewise esential to Christian prayer. And this communal quality of our prayer finds graphic expression not only in the Lord's Prayer, but, as we shall see, in the prayer of the Church.

CHAPTER 7

# THE PRAYER OF THE CHURCH

## Unity in Multiplicity

INSOFAR AS CHRIST is the source from which we receive the life of grace, he is, from that point of view, the "Father" of our supernatural life. But if he be the "Father" of a supernatural family, he must have a bride; and it is the Church that is chosen as the spouse of Christ. Through her he brings us forth to the life of grace, builds himself a family that shall grow into a great people — the city of God. "We had a father and mother on earth that we might be born to labor and death; but we have found other parents: God our Father and the Church our Mother, by whom we are born unto life everlasting."[1] There were two things, according to Augustine, that our Divine Lord loved above all others on this earth: his mother and his Church. "Mary mothered your leader," preached Augustine; "the Church mothered you; for she also is mother and virgin. Mother through the womb of her charity; virgin in the integrity of her faith and of her piety. She issues to the world entire peoples, but they are all members of a single Christ, of which she is the body and the spouse. One can say of her as of Mary: She is the mother of unity in multiplicity."[2]

The comparison according to which the Church appears as an interior and spiritual society of souls, linked directly to the Incarnate Word as to its chief, is inspired by the Gospel, in which Christ said to his apostles: *Live on in me, as I do in you. No more than a branch can bear fruit of itself apart from the vine, can you bear fruit apart from me* (John 15:4). This organic unity is again explicitly affirmed by Saint Paul. *The body is one and has many members, but all the members, many though they are, are one body; and so it is with Christ. It was in one Spirit that all of us, whether Jew or Greek, slave or free, were baptized into one body. All of us have been given to drink of one Spirit* (1 Corinthians 12:12-13). This unity in multiplicity, this oneness of his members with himself, was the theme of the Savior's prayer at the Last Supper. *I do not pray for them alone. I pray also for those who will believe in me through their word, that all may be one as you, Father, are in me, and I in you; I pray that they may be [one] in us, that the world may believe that you sent me. I have given them the glory you gave me that they may be one, as we are one* (John 17:20-22).

The Church, then, is not just a society of many members, however numerous; nor is it merely an external organization united by the will to pursue the same common good. Its unity is that of a single, living organism, like a vine; or like that of a single, living person. It must not be equated with the worldwide association of all Christian souls, as if it were the sum of all Christian personalities, created by their voluntary federation, and dependent on their good pleasure for its continued existence. The Church is antecedent to all Christian personalities; it does not presuppose them, it creates and produces them. It is not the branches that give life to the vine; it is the vine that gives life to the branches. "Therefore, all of us, together with our head, *we are Christ:* without our head we are worth nothing. Why? Because, together with our head we are the vine; without our head — which God forbid — we are lopped-off branches, destined to do no work for the Husbandman, but for the fire only. So he himself says in the Gospel: *I am the vine, you are the branches. He who lives in me and I in him, will produce abundantly, for apart from me you can do nothing* (John 15:5)."[3] Being engrafted into this vine which is Christ, is the very condition of our spiritual life and of our supernatural fruitfulness.

"When I call Christians many," declares Augustine, "I understand them to be one in Christ."[4] So we are many, and we are one. "He is one, we are many; he is one, and we are one in him."[5] "We are one because Christ is one and we are his members."[6] "Our Lord Jesus Christ, like a whole and perfect man, is head and body . . . The body of this head is the Church; and not just the Church in this particular place, but both the Church that is here, and the Church that extends itself over the whole earth; and not only the Church that is living today, but the whole race of saints, from Abel down to all those who will ever be born, and who will believe in Christ to the end of the world. For all belong to one city. This city is the body of Christ . . . This is the whole Christ: Christ united to his Church."[7] "Let us rejoice and give thanks. Not only are we become Christians, we are become Christ! My brethren, do you understand the grace that is given us? Marvel, rejoice, for we are made Christ! If he be the head and if we be the members, then, he and we together are the whole man . . . This would be foolish pride on our part were it not a gift of his bounty. But this is what he promised by the lips of his Apostle: *You, then, are the body of Christ. Every one of you is a member of it* (1 Corinthians 12:27)."[8]

While emphasizing the intimacy of the union between Christ and his members, however, Augustine clearly maintains certain distinctions. "We do not separate the two realities," he says, "though we do distinguish two different dignities: For the head saves, the body is saved."[9] Furthermore, it is not Christ as the Word of God who is the head of the Church. "The Word is made flesh in order to become the head of the Church. Because the Word himself is not a part of the Church; but in order to become the head he has taken a body."[10] In this way he preserves his own personal activities, those of his divine life, in spite of the intimacy of his union with his members. It is not the Word, or divinity as such, that is the head of the Church, but the Word made flesh. Consequently, though he as their head condescends to be what his members are, it does not follow that they are what he is as the second person of the Blessed Trinity, that is, God. Nevertheless, the Word Incarnate is "human divinity and divine humanity,"[11] and even as the humanity of Christ was sanctified through its assumption by the Word, so are the members of Christ sanctified in their head.

"Since, then, he is the Mediator of God and men, the man Christ Jesus has been made head of the Church, and the faithful are his members. Wherefore, he says: *I consecrate myself for their sakes now* (John 17:19): And when he says this, what else does he mean but, 'I sanctify them in myself, since truly they are myself'? For, as I have already remarked, those of whom he speaks are his members, and head and body are one Christ. That he signifies this unity is certain from what follows in the same verse. For having said: 'For them do I hallow myself,' he immediately adds: 'that they also may be sanctified in truth.' Now, the words, 'in truth,' can only mean, 'in me,' since truth is the Word who in the beginning was God. The Son of Man was himself sanctified in the Word at the moment of his creation, when the Word was made flesh, for Word and man became one person. It was at that instant, therefore, that he hallowed himself, that is, that he hallowed himself as man in himself as the Word. For there is but one Christ, Word and man, sanctifying himself in the Word. But now it is on behalf of his members that he adds: 'and for them do I hallow myself.' That is to say, that since they too are myself, so they too may profit by this sanctification, just as I profited by it as man without them. 'And for them do I hallow myself': that is, I sanctify them in myself as myself, since they too are myself."[12]

This very manifest desire of the Son of God made man to identify us with himself, should not surprise us. For God is love; and love not only creates more love, it strives to unite those who love each other. "What is love, if not a certain life which unifies, or seeks to unify, two things, namely, him that loves and that which is loved?"[13] Christ, therefore, has identified the Church with himself so that they are one person, one man, one body, the whole Christ — the unity in which we love and pray. "He wills his own to be one," says Augustine, "but in himself . . . that they may be one in him, not only through the same nature in which all from being mortal men are made equal to the angels, but also through the same will harmoniously conspiring to the same happiness, and fused in some way by the fire of charity into one spirit."[14] We have seen that love and prayer are gifts from God, and that the love which *is* God is *poured out in our hearts through the Holy Spirit who has been given to us* (Romans 5:5). Now this Holy Spirit is the very soul of the Mystical Body of Christ, because "the body of Christ cannot live but by the spirit of Christ,"[15] and if we would live by this spirit, we must be members of that body in which the spirit dwells, and through which it communicates itself.

We are all one in Christ, as the body and soul are one in a single living man. For though we be many, we all live by the same life, and we are unified by the same Holy Spirit that dwells in us, just as all the members of a body are given unison of life and harmony and of operation by the indwelling soul. "See what the soul does in the body. It feeds all the members; it gives life to all; and it gives to each member the function proper to it. The eye does not hear, the ear does not see, nevertheless, it lives. The functions vary, but the life is common to all. So it is with the Church of God. There are priests and laity, virgins and married people, each having their own proper activity, but all having the same spiritual life. Now, what the soul is to the human body, the Holy Spirit is to the body of Christ which is the Church. He accomplishes in the whole Church what the soul does in all the members of a single body."[16] Through the Mystical Body of Christ, therefore, the Savior communicates his life and his holiness to us, and in so doing he communicates his love and his prayer. And this love which is poured forth in our hearts must be, not only affective, but effective; and to be effective it must be operative — it must express itself in prayer.

## The Unity That Prays

"Let the members of Christ understand. Let them see Christ in his members, and the members of Christ in Christ; for head and members are one Christ."[17] It was the will of God that Christ and the Church should be one. *And the two shall be made into one.* said Saint Paul. *This is a great foreshadowing; I mean that it refers to Christ and the church* (Romans 5:2). "And if they be two in one flesh," queries Augustine, "why not two in one voice?"[18] For if they be one, then, the Church speaks in Christ, and Christ speaks in the Church: the body in the head, and the head in the body. "Even though absent from our eyes, Christ our head is bound to us by love. And since the whole Christ is head and body, let us listen to the voice of the head in such a manner that we may also hear the body speak. He no more wished to speak alone than he wished to exist alone, for he says: *And know that I am with you always until the end of the world!* (Matthew 28:20). If he is with us, then, he speaks in us, he speaks for us, he speaks through us; and we also speak in him."[19]

Augustine tells us that he found it difficult to find any voices in the Psalms except those of Christ and the Church. "Sometimes," he says, "it is the voice of Christ alone, and sometimes it is that of the Church alone, of which we certainly are members."[20] "The members of the Church, many though they be, are bound to one another by the ties of charity and of peace under the one head, who is our Savior himself, and they form one man. The voice of the many is frequently heard in the Psalms as the voice of one man; the cry of one is as the cry of all, for all in one are one."[21] "And because we are many, the Scriptures say that we praise God altogether (*collaudamus*); and because we are one, it says that each of us praise him (*laudamus*). The same who are many are one; for he is ever one in whom we are one."[22]

"Consequently, when we speak to God in prayer for mercy, we do not separate the Son from him; and when the body of the Son prays it does not separate itself from the head. It is the one Savior of his body, our Lord Jesus Christ, who prays both for us and in us, and is prayed to by us. He prays for us as our priest; he prays in us as our head; he is prayed to by us as our God. Let us, then, acknowledge our words in him, and his words in us . . . He is prayed to in the form of God; he prays in the form of a servant. In the first case he is the Creator; in the latter he is 'created,' the unchanging assuming the form of a creature that the creature may be changed, and so making us with himself, one man, head and body . . . Be unwilling to say anything without him, and he will say nothing without you."[23]

Sometimes, then, Christ speaks as our head, and at other times he speaks and prays on behalf of his members. "This is the case," observes Augustine, "in that Psalm, the first verse of which the Lord himself spoke from the cross: *My God, my God, why have you forsaken me?* (Psalm 22:2). Transferring us into what he was saying, and into his body — for we also are his body and he is our head — he uttered our cry from the cross, not his own. Because God never forsook him; nor did he himself ever depart from the Father. So it was on our behalf that he uttered the words: *My God, my God, why have you forsaken me?* (Matthew 27:46). Moreover, note the words that follow after: *Far from my prayer, from the words of my cry?* (Psalm 22:2). This verse shows in whose person he spoke the preceding words, for sin could find no place in him."[24] "Sometimes, then, he speaks as our head, and at other times he speaks for us who are his members. When he said: *For I was hungry and you gave me food* (Matthew 25:35), he spoke for his members, and not on his own behalf. And when he said: *Saul, Saul, why do you persecute me?* (Acts 9:4), it was the head crying out on behalf of its members. Yet, he did not say: 'Why do you persecute my members,' but, *Why do you persecute me?* If he suffers in us, then we also shall be crowned in him. Such is the love of Christ. Can anything be compared to this?"[25] "The Church suffered in him, when he suffered for the Church; just as he suffered in the Church, when the Church suffered for his sake. For just as we have heard the voice of the Church suffering in Christ: *My God, my God, why have you forsaken me?* so also have we heard the voice of Christ suffering in the Church: *Saul, Saul, why do you persecute me?*"[26]

"Why, then, do we disdain to hear the voice of the body from the mouth of the head?"[27] His prayer is our prayer, and our prayer is his prayer — provided we do not cut ourselves off from him. "Therefore, as soon as our head begins to pray, let us understand that we are in him, that so we may share our prayer with him just as we share in his tribulation."[28] The prayer of all is as the prayer of one man; and this one man can address the Lord and say: *From the earth's end I call to you* (Psalm 61:3). "If we are his members and in his body — as we are bold enough to believe on his exhortation — then, we should acknowledge the voice in this psalm as our own and not that of any stranger. I have not called it our own as if it were that of those of us who are now here present, but of all of us spread through the whole world from the east even to the west. And that you may know it is our voice, he speaks in this psalm as if with the voice of one man; but like a single man, it is the unity that is speaking. In Christ we are all one man; and the head of this one man is in heaven while the members are still toiling on the earth. And because they are toiling, see what he says: *Hear, O God, my cry; listen to my prayer! From the earth's end I call you as my heart grows faint* (Psalm 61:2-3) . . . But what one man cries from the ends of the earth? Nothing cries from the ends of the earth save that inheritance concerning which it was said to the Son himself, *Ask of me and I will give you the nations for an inheritance and the ends of the earth for your possession* (Psalm 2:8). This inheritance of Christ, this body of Christ, this one Church of Christ, this unity to which we belong, is crying from the ends of the earth."[29]

"Let him rise up, this one chanter; let this man sing from the heart of each of us, and let each one of us be in this man. When each of you sings a verse it is still this one man that sings, since you are all one in Christ. We do not say, 'To you, O Lord, we lift up our eyes,' but *To you I lift up my eyes* (Psalm 123:1). You should of course consider that each of you is speaking, but that primarily this one man is speaking who reaches to the end of the earth."[30] "How can this one man cry out from the ends of the earth unless he be one in all?"[31]

## "One Thing I Have Asked of the Lord"

The end of all Christian endeavor, and the object of all Christian prayer, is to see God face to face in the kingdom of his glory. This will be the reward of the pilgrim's love. And in order to attain this neverending end, we must adhere to Christ so as to be one with him even on this earth. Augustine observes that, "Our Lord Jesus Christ himself said: *No one has come up to heaven except the One who came down from there — the Son of Man [who is in heaven]* (John 3:13). And he seems to have spoken of himself only. If, then, he alone ascends who alone descended, have all others been left behind? What must these others do? They must be united with his body, so that there may be but One Christ who descends and ascends. The head descended, and he ascends with his body; he ascends clothed with the Church which he has presented to himself without spot or wrinkle (cf. Ephesians 5:27). In this way he still ascends alone. For when we are so united with him as to be his members, then even with us he is alone, and therefore one — always one."[32]

Saint Augustine exhorts us, therefore, to stand fast in the faith, and to be loyal to our holy Mother the Church, in all the temptations of life. The history of the Mystical Body was graphically summarized by Saint Matthew when he said: *Meanwhile the boat, already several hundred yards out from shore, was being tossed about in the waves raised by strong headwinds* (Matthew 14:24). "By the very nature of the journey we are exposed to waves and tempests; so it is necessary that we be at least *in* the ship." "If there be danger on board ship, there is instant disaster outside of it . . . And even though the ship be in difficulty, still it *is* the ship . . . Keep yourself safely on board, then, and pray to God. For when all counsels fail, when the very helm is unserviceable, and the spreading of sail more hazardous than helpful, when all human help and strength have been exhausted, then, for those on board, there remains only the earnest cry of entreaty, and the pouring forth of prayers to God. And shall he, who grants that sailors reach their haven, so forsake his Church as not to lead it on to rest!"[33]

*One thing I ask of the Lord; this I seek: to dwell in the house of the Lord all the days of my life, that I may gaze on the loveliness of the Lord and contemplate his temple* (Psalm 27:4). "In order that we may attain this happy life, he who is himself the true Blessed Life has taught us to pray."[34] But what shall we do now, during this our life and pilgrimage? "Let us sigh now; let us pray now. Sighs belong to the miserable; prayers belong to those in need. Prayers shall pass away and praise shall take their place; tears shall pass away to be replaced with joy. Meanwhile, during these evil days let us never cease from making that petition until, by his grace and guidance, we have attained to it."[35] "In the midst of our wanderings here, we are hurt at times; but our last home shall be a home of joy alone. Hard work, sighs, and prayers shall pass away, to be succeeded by hymns of praise . . . For he shall be with us for whom we sigh, and, *We shall be like him, for we shall see him as he is* (1 John 3:2) . . . Prepare yourselves for a certain ineffable delight; cleanse your hearts from all earthly and mundane affections. We will see something, the vision of which shall make us happy, something which shall alone suffice us."[36] "We shall see God. And that shall be so great, so stupendous a reality, that in comparison with it, all else shall be as nothing."[37] "We shall be like him, for we shall see him as he is." "The tongue has done what it could; it has spoken the words. Let the rest be pondered in the heart."[38]

"It will repay us, then, to inquire after and to discuss in detail what we are going to do in that home, for which we express our hope and desire when we repeat the words, *One thing I ask of the Lord.* What shall we do in that home in which we hope to dwell all the days of our lives? Listen: *that I may gaze on the loveliness of the Lord.* That is what I love; and that is why I wish to live in the house of the Lord all the days of my life. What a glorious vision will be presented to us in the gazing on the loveliness of the Lord!"[39] We shall see God. "And so charming is the face of God, that once it is seen, nothing else shall ever give delight."[40] "There we shall rest and we shall see; we shall see and we shall love; we shall love and we shall praise."[41] Such will be the activity of the elect: contemplation, love, and praise.

*Happy they who dwell in your house!* (Psalm 84:5). But why? *Continually they praise you* (Psalm 84:5). "Such will be our activity, the praise of God. You love and you praise. You would cease to love if you ceased to praise. But you will never cease to love because he whom you shall see will never weary you."[42] Such is the reward of the pilgrim's love. He shall rest in the Lord; he shall gaze on the loveliness of the Lord; he shall love and praise the Lord. He shall rejoice in "the everlasting reign of those who perfectly praise him because they see him face to face."[43] "There is praise given to God, and here on earth is praise given to God; but here by those full of anxious care, there by those who are free from care; here by those whose lot it is to die, there by those who are to live forever; here in hope, there in hope realized; here on the way, there in our Fatherland. Now, therefore, my brethren, let us sing, not for delight as we rest, but to cheer us in our labor. As pilgrims are wont to sing, sing, but travel on!"[44]

Meanwhile, as they walk the pilgrim's way, men must be careful of what they love and of what they ask in prayer. "Men have many things," observes Augustine, "and when a man seems to have what he loves, he is called happy. But he is truly happy, not if he has what he loves, but if he loves what he ought to love. Many are more miserable in having what they love than in wanting it. For men who are miserable through loving hurtful things are rendered more miserable still by possessing them . . . This is the one petition that ought to be loved — that we may dwell in the house of the Lord all the days of our life."[45] "Whoever desires that one thing of the Lord and seeks after it, asks with certainty and with confidence, and has no fear that when it is obtained it may be harmful to him, seeing that without it anything else he may have acquired through praying as he ought is of no advantage to him. The thing referred to is the one true and only happy life in which, immortal and incorruptible in body and in spirit, we may contemplate the joy of the Lord forever. All other things are desired and are prayed for without impropriety, with a view to this one thing."[46]

The whole life of a Christian should be a holy desire for this truly happy life, "for a person lives in those things which he loves, which he greatly desires, and in which he believes himself to be happy."[47] This desire, moreover, will enlarge the soul until it is capable of receiving everlasting happiness. "By desiring you open up and expand the soul, by expanding it you make it capable of receiving more. Let us stretch ourselves unto him, so that when he shall come he may fill our souls."[48] This should be our unceasing desire, our unceasing prayer. "What else is intended by the words of the Apostle: *Pray without ceasing,* if not, 'Desire without ceasing, from him who alone can give it, a happy life, which no life can be but that which is eternal'? This, therefore, let us desire without intermission from the Lord our God, and so let us pray without ceasing."[49] "This is the final blessedness, this is the ultimate consummation, this is the unending end."[50]

## Amen. Alleluia!

Eternal life will be the last Amen, the final Alleluia, that shall be neverending. "And it is not with the fleeting echoes of our voices that we shall then be saying, 'Amen' and 'Alleluia,' but with the affectionate feelings of the heart."[51] Alleluia means the praise of God. "To us as we labor," says Augustine, "it signifies the activity of our eternal rest. For when, after these labors, we come to that rest, the praise of God will be our sole occupation. Our activity there will be 'Alleluia' . . . our food will be 'Alleluia'; our drink will be 'Alleluia'; our whole joy will be 'Alleluia' — the praise of God."[52] "Today, hope sings it, and sometimes love. But then love alone shall sing it. The love that sometimes sings it in this life is a love of desire, whereas it will then be sung by a love that rejoices in the everlasting possession of its beloved."[53] Such will be the Sabbath of life everlasting, in which the only ultimate happiness open to man will be forever realized.

"There shall peace be made perfect in the sons of God all loving one another, seeing one another possessed of God, since God shall be all in all. We shall have God as our common vision, God as our common possession, God as our common peace. And whatever there is that he gives us here and now, he himself will be in place of all his gifts. He will be our full and perfect peace . . . Our peace, our rest, our joy, the end of all our troubles, is none but God."[54] The Savior has transformed us into a new race. He has put a new canticle into our mouths — a song to our God.[55] We are pilgrims homeward bound, as we *sing praise to the Lord with all our hearts* (Ephesians 5:19). "O sons of peace, sons of the one, Catholic Church, walk in your way, and sing as you walk. Travelers do this to keep up their spirits. Do you also sing on the way. I beseech you, by the very way in which you walk, sing on this road, sing the new canticle. Let no one sing old songs, but sing the songs of love of your country; let none sing the old. For the way is new, the traveler is new, and the song is new."[56]

*Turning, then, to the Lord our God, let us as best we can give thanks with all our hearts, beseeching him that in his goodness he would mercifully hear our prayers, and by his grace drive evil from our thoughts and actions, increase our faith, grant us his holy inspirations, and lead us to neverending joy, through his Son, our Lord and Savior Jesus Christ. Amen.*[57]

# NOTES

## CHAPTER 1

1 Sermon 306, 3.
2 Ibid. 3.
3 Sermon 150, 4.
4 Ibid. 4.
5 Ibid. 4.
6 Cf. Sermon 345, 5.
7 Cf. Letter 130, 12.
8 Cf. *Trinity,* XIII, iv, 7.
9 Cf. *Against the Academics,* I, ii, 5.
10 Cf. *Trinity,* XIII, iv, 7.
11 Cf. *City of God,* VIII, 4.
12 *Trinity,* VIII, iv, 6.
13 *Confessions,* IV, xiii, 20.
14 *City of God,* XIV, 7.
15 Ibid. XIV, 7 — "Id autem habens eoque fruens, laetitia est."
16 *Confessions,* XIII, xi, 10.
17 Ibid. 10.
18 Letter 55, 18 — "Donec ad locum quo nititur veniens, requiescat."
19 Ibid. 18.
20 On Ps. 31 — 2nd — 6.
21 Cf. *On Free Will,* III, i, 2 — "Lapidi naturalis est ille motus, animo vero iste voluntarius."
22 Cf. Tr. on John XXVI, 4 — "Non necessitas, sed voluptas; non obligatio, sed delectatio."
23 Tr. on John XLI, 10 — "Libertas enim delectat."
24 *Trinity,* XIII, iv, 7.
25 Cf. *Confessions,* IV, xiv, 22.
26 On Ps. 32 — 2nd — 5.
27 Cf. On Ps. 2, II — "Ubi est bonorum omnium summa et cumulus."
28 Cf. Letter 130, 10.
29 Ibid. II; cf. *Trinity,* XIII, v, 8.
30 *Morals of Cath. Chur.* III, 4.
31 Letter 118, 13.
32 *Morals of Cath. Chur.* III, 4.
33 Letter 118, 13.
34 Letter 118, 14.
35 Ibid. 13.
36 Sermon 150, 8.
37 Cf. *Confessions,* XIII, viii, 9.
38 *On the Happy Life,* 11 — "Deum igitur, inquam, qui habet, beatus est."
39 *On the True Religion,* XI, 21.
40 Ibid.
41 *City of God,* XI, 13.
42 *Morals of Cath. Chur.,* XI, 18.
43 Cf. Sermon 34, 7 — "Totum exigit te, qui fecit te."
44 *Morals of Cath. Chur.,* VI, 10.
45 *Confessions,* I, i, 1.
46 *On the Nature of Good,* VII.
47 *Morals of Cath. Chur.* VIII, 13.
48 *Morals of Cath. Chur.* XI, 18.
49 *Morals of Cath. Chur.* XIV, 24.
50 *Christian Doct.* I, XII, 21.
51 *Various Questions,* 83, 35 — "Talis est quisque, qualis ejus dilectio est."
52 Cf. Ibid. 35.
53 *Christian Doct.* III, x, 16 — "Caritatem voco motum animi ad fruendum Deum propter Ipsum."
54 Sermon 9 (de Passione), 3 — "Oratio namque est mentis ad Deum affectuosa intentio."
55 On Ps. 37, 14.
56 Sermon 91, 3.
57 Ibid. 3.
58 On Ps. 118 — 29th — 1.
59 Tr. on 1 John IV, 6.
60 On Ps. 86, 1.
61 On Ps. 102, 8.
62 On Ps. 119, 9.
63 On Ps. 3, 4.
64 On Ps. 139, 10.
65 On Ps. 118 — 29th — 1.
66 Letter 130, 18.
67 *The Teacher,* 1, 2.
68 Sermon 80, 2.
69 Sermon 56, 4; cf. also Letter 140, "Pius mentis affectus est, ut ipsa construantur non ut Deus instruantur."
70 Serm. on Mount, 11, iii, 13.
71 *The Teacher,* 1, 2.
72 Sermon 56, 4.
73 Letter 130, 17.

74 *Christian Doct.* I, iii, 3.
75 Ibid.
76 Letter 130, 24.
77 Letter 130, 15 — "Propter hanc adipiscendam vitam beatam ipsa vera Vita beata nos orare docuit . . ."
78 *The Trinity,* XIII, vii, 10.
79 Cf. 1 Cor. 15, 53.
80 Letter 130, 7.
81 *The Trinity,* XIII, vii, 10.
82 Ibid.
83 On Ps. 91, 1.
84 On Ps. 90 — 1st — 7.
85 *The Trinity,* XIII, viii, 11.
86 Letter 130, 27.
87 *The Trinity,* XIII, viii, 11.
88 Ibid.
89 Ibid. 12.
90 Ibid.
91 On Ps. 148, 8.
92 On Ps. 26 — 1st — 8, 9.
93 Letter 130, 15.

CHAPTER 2

1 Tr. on John CX:6.
2 Letter 11:4.
3 *Confessions,* VII,xviii:24.
4 *On Catech. the Uninstructed,* IV:7.
5 Trinity IV,i:2.
6 See On 1 John Tr. VII:9.
7 Letter 127:1.
8 *City of God,* VII:31.
9 Sermon 57:13.
10 Sermon 141:1; *Ibid.* 4.
11 Against letter of Fundatus, 36:41.
12 *The Christian Combat,* I,xi:12.
13 On Psalm 56:5.
14 Sermon 61:1-3.
15 Sermon 105:1.
16 Letter 130:15.
17 Tr. on John 104:2.
18 On Psalm 29 — 2nd — 1.
19 Tr. on John 93:1.
20 *The Trinity,* XV,xvi:27.
21 See *The Trinity,* XV,xix:37.
22 See *Ibid.* XV,xvii:31.
23 *The Trinity,* XV,xviii:32.
24 Sermon 297:1 "Amare Deum Dei donum est."
25 Sermon 34:2. sq. — "Amemus Deum de Deo."
26 Sermon 156:16.
27 Sermon 128:4.
28 *The Trinity,* XV,xvii:31.
29 Letter 147:44 — "Ecce etiam caritas quantulacumque in nostra voluntate consistit . . ."
30 *Grace of Christ,* 1,xxi:22.
31 *Christian Doct.* III,x:16.
32 On Psalm 118 — 17th — 2.
33 Sermon 61:6.
34 Tr. on John XXVI:4.
35 Letter 130:17.
36 Sermon on Mount II,iii:4.
37 Tr. on John XXVI:4.
38 See *Christian Doct.* II,viii:9-11.
39 *The Trinity,* XV,xix:34.
40 Sermon 168:5.
41 *Ibid.* 6.
42 Letter 194:16.
43 Gift of Perseverance, 64.
44 Letter 194:18.
45 *The Trinity,* VIII,iv:6.
46 Tr. on John II:4.
57 Sermon 43:1.
48 *On the Spirit and Letter,* XXXVI:64 — "Quanto magis notitia, tanto erit maior dilectio."
49 See Tr. on 1 John IV:4.
50 See Sermon 118:1 — "Praecedit fides, sequitur intellectus."
51 See Sermon 126:1 — "Fides enim gradus est intelligendi; intellectus autem meritum fidei."
52 *The Trinity,* XV,ii:2.
53 Sermon 115:1.
54 *Enchiridion,* VII.
55 Sermon 158:7 — "Fides enim quae per dilectionem operatur, sine spe esse non potest."

56 Sermon 53:11.
57 *Ibid.* 53:11 — "Contristat nos quia non videmus."
58 See *Christian Doct.* I,xxxviii:42.
59 See *Soliloquies,* I,xiv:15.
60 Letter 130:2.
61 On Psalm 31 — 2nd — 5.
62 On Psalm 65 — 1st — 24.

CHAPTER 3

1 Letter 171(a):1.
2 Sermon 19:6.
3 *On Correction and Grace,* 2.
4 Letter 188:8.
5 *Confessions,* X,xxi:45.
6 *Grace and Free-Will,* 32.
7 *Ibid.* 33.
8 On Psalm 118 — 17th — 3:4.
9 On Psalm 118 — 27th — 4.
10 *On Man's Perfection in Righteousness,* X:21.
11 *Ibid.*
12 *City of God,* X:22.
13 *On Nature and Grace,* 80.
14 *On Various Questions to Simplicanus,* I,ii:18.
15 *On Free Will,* II:53.
16 On Psalm 145:5.
17 Letter 177:4.
18 On Psalm 30 — 3rd — 2.
19 *On Nature and Grace,* 68.
20 *On Man's Perfection in Righteousness,* xxi:44.
21 *On Nature and Grace,* 65.
22 On Psalm 55:2.
23 Sermon 2:3.
24 On Psalm 63:1.
25 *Sermon on the Mount,* II,ix:34.
26 On Psalm 118 — 26th — 2.
27 *On Grace and Free Will,* 9.
28 *On Man's Perfection in Righteousness,* xx:43.
29 *Ibid.* 40.
30 *The Excellence of Widowhood,* xvii:21.
31 Letter 145:8.
32 Letter 189:2.
33 *On Nature and Grace,* 68.
34 *Ibid.*
35 *Ibid.* 71.
36 Letter 167:15.
37 On Psalm 91:1.
38 Tr. on 1 John v:4.
39 Sermon 344:1.
40 On Psalm 109:1.
41 *On the Spirit and Letter,* 7.
42 On Psalm 89:17.
43 Tr. on 1 John vii:1.
44 *On Man's Perfection in Righteousness,* viii:18.
45 See *Sermon on the Mount,* II,xi:38.
46 On Psalm 38:6.
47 *On Man's Perfection in Righteousness,* viii:19.
48 *On Questions,* 31.
49 *Gift of Perseverance,* 1.
50 Sermon 75:6.
51 *Gift of Perseverance,* 39.
52 *On Correction and Grace,* 10.
53 *Gift of Perseverance,* 63.
54 On Psalm 75:16.
55 On Psalm 130:14.
56 On Psalm 83:4.
57 Sermon 38:4.
58 Sermon 256:3.
59 On Psalm 56:2.

CHAPTER 4

1 Cf. Letter 130, 12-13.
2 *Christian Doct.* I, xxvii, 28.
3 Sermon 368, 5.
4 Letter 155, 13.
5 Sermon 368, 4.
6 Letter 155, 15.
7 *On Christian Discipline,* 3.
8 Sermon 368, 5.

9 *The Trinity,* XIV, 18.
10 Ibid. VIII, 12.
11 On Ps. 85, 8.
12 On Ps. 26 — 2nd — 19.
13 On Ps. 76, 2.
14 On Ps. 52, 8.
15 On Ps. 30 — 3rd — 4.
16 Ibid. 4.
17 On Ps. 76, 2.
18 Tr. on 1 John, ii, 11.
19 Sermon 91, 3.
20 Sermon 331, 4.
21 Sermon 304, 3 — "Hoc est Deum gratis amare, de Deo Deum sperare . . ."
22 On Ps. 39, 7-8.
23 *Confessions,* IV, xii, 18.
24 On Ps. 53, 10.
25 On Ps. 72, 32.
26 Sermon 113, 6 — "Fac nos beatos de Te, quia non perdemus Te."
27 On Ps. 40,3.
28 *The Nature of Good,* 34.
29 Cf. Sermon 91, 3.
30 Sermon 159, 2.
31 Letter 130, 12.
32 Ibid. 12-13.
33 Sermon 61, 3.
34 Ibid. 2.
35 Letter 130, 3.
36 Sermon 21, 9.
37 Letter 15, 2.
38 Letter 140, 3.
39 Letter 140, 2-3.
40 *Sermon on Mount,* II, xvi, 53.
41 Letter 130, 3 — "Inde necesse est fiat homo beatus unde fit bonus."
42 *City of God,* XIX, 13.
43 On Ps. 64, 14.
44 On Ps. 32 — 2nd — 16.
45 Sermon 80, 7.
46 On Ps. 26 — 2nd — 5.
47 Tr. on John 65, 2.
48 Cf. On Ps. 14, 3 — "Proximum omnem hominem accipi oportere necesse est."
49 On Ps. 118 — 8th — 2.
50 *Christian Doct.* I, xxviii, 29.
51 *Christian Doct.* I, xxix, 30.
52 *City of God,* XV, 5.
53 On Ps. 49, 2.
54 On Ps. 54, 4.
55 On Ps. 39, 11. Cf. also On Ps. 73, 34 — "Love God gratis: Grudge him to no one."
56 Sermon 17, 2.
57 Letter 170, 10.
58 *Morals of Catholic Church,* xxvi, 49.
59 *Confessions,* IV, xiv, 21 — "Ex amante alio incenditur alius."
60 Tr. on John 65, 2.
61 Tr. on 1 John 1, 8.
62 Tr. on 1 John x, 8.
63 Sermon 168, 6.
64 Cf. Letter 217, 2.
65 *Gift of Perseverance,* 66.
66 Tr. on 1 John 1, 9.
67 Sermon 90, 10 — "Rape, rape inimicum, rapiendo non erit inimicum."
68 Tr. on 1 John 1, 9.
69 On Ps. 37, 14.
70 On Ps. 138, 28.
71 Cf. On Ps. 33 — 2nd — 9.
72 On Ps. 39, 4.
73 Sermon 9, 9.
74 On Ps. 32 — 2nd — 1.
75 Sermon 149, 16.
76 Sermon 90, 9.
77 Cf. Tr. on 1 John 8, 9 — "Opta illi ut habeat tecum vitam aeternam."
78 Sermon 90, 10.
79 *Confessions,* IX, xi, 27.
80 Ibid. IX, xiii, 35-37.
81 Ibid. IX, xi, 28.
82 *Care of the Dead,* IV, 6.
83 Cf. Ibid. V, 7.
84 Ibid. IV, 6.
85 Sermon 172, 2.
86 *Care of the Dead,* XVIII, 22.
87 Ibid. III, 5.
88 Sermon 172, 2.
89 *Care of the Dead,* I, 3.

90 Ibid. IV, 6.
91 Ibid. XVIII, 22.
92 *Enchiridion,* 110.
93 Ibid.
94 *Care of the Dead,* XVIII, 22.
95 Cf. Ephesians 5, 29.
96 *Care of the Dead,* XVIII, 22.
97 Sermon 172, 3.
98 Sermon 172, 1.
99 Sermon 173, 3.
100 *Confessions,* IX, xii, 32.
101 Saint Ambrose — "Deus Creator omnium." Tr. published 1660; author unknown.

CHAPTER 5

1 On Ps. 148 — 2nd — 1.
2 Sermon 210, 9.
3 Sermon 56, 5.
4 On Ps. 93, 1.
5 On Ps. 30 — 3rd — 10.
6 On Ps. 141, 2.
7 On Ps. 85, 10.
8 *Confessions,* I, v, 6.
9 On Ps. 33, — 2nd — 8.
10 On Ps. 144, 22.
11 On Ps. 43, 16.
12 On Ps. 52, 8.
13 On Ps. 77, 21.
14 Ibid.
15 On Ps. 39, 7.
16 Sermon 87, 1.
17 On Ps. 59, 7.
18 Tr. on John, 73, 3.
19 Ibid. 73, 4.
20 Tr. on John, 102, 2.
21 *On the Spirit and Letter,* 63.
22 Sermon 131, 2.
23 On Ps. 30 — 3rd — 10.
24 *City of God,* II, 28.
25 *Catech. the Uninstructed,* 39.
26 Sermon 33, 3.
27 Sermon 158, 7.
28 On Ps. 42, 2.
29 On Ps. 118 — 14th — 2.
30 Tr. on John, 15, 7.
31 Sermon 165, 4.
32 Sermon 83, 2 — "Omnes enim quando oramus mendici Dei sumus."
33 *Rule,* 10, 3.
34 Sermon 83, 7.
35 Sermon 58, 10.
36 On Ps. 103 — 1st — 19.
37 Ibid.
38 Sermon 83, 3.
39 Sermon 83, 3-4.
40 *Rule,* 10, 2.
41 Letter 140, 42.
42 Sermon 115, 2.
43 Ibid.
44 Sermon 45, 7.
45 Cf. On Ps. 93, 15.
46 On Ps. 45, 14.
47 Sermon 169, 11.
48 On Ps. 93, 15.
49 Letter 232, 6.
50 Sermon 190, 4.
51 Sermon 188, 2.
52 *Christian Combat,* XI, 12.
53 Tr. on John, XXV, 16.
54 On Ps. 90 — 1st — 1.
55 Sermon 97, 2.
56 Tr. on John, XXV, 16.
57 On Ps. 135, 1.
58 Sermon 13, 2.
59 On Ps. 38, 18.
60 On Ps. 118 — 2nd — 1.
61 Tr. on 1 John, 1, 6.
62 On Ps. 85, 2.
63 On Ps. 145, 4.
64 Ibid. 5.
65 *Confessions,* VIII, ix, 21.
66 Letter 130, 20.
67 On Ps. 85, 6.
68 *Rule,* 3, 2.
69 On Ps. 30 — 3rd — 1.

70 On Ps. 85, 7.
71 On Ps. 145, 6.
72 Ibid.
73 On Ps. 85, 7.
74 Ibid.
75 On Ps. 140, 18.
76 On Ps. 85, 7.
77 Ibid.
78 Sermon 105, 2-3.
79 On Ps. 102, 10.
80 Sermon 61, 6.
81 Sermon 80, 7.
82 Sermon 80, 2 — "Quid enim desideres tu nosti; quid tibi prosit, ille novit."
83 On Ps. 144, 19.
84 Sermon 354, 7.
85 Tr. on John, LXXIII, 1.
86 Letter 130, 26.
87 Tr. on John, XX, 3.
88 Sermon 61, 6.
89 On Ps. 87, 14.
90 On Ps. 41, 17.
91 Sermon 9 (de Passione), 3.
92 On Ps. 34 — 2nd — 16.
93 Letter 130, 19.
94 On Ps. 34 — 2nd — 16.
95 On Ps. 148, 2.

## CHAPTER 6

1 Tr. on John 7, 2.
2 Letter 130, 21.
3 Ibid., 24.
4 Letter 130, 22.
5 Ibid., 22.
6 Ibid.
7 Sermon 56, 4.
8 Sermon 56, 2.
9 Letter 130, 23.
10 *Sermon on Mount,* II, 26.
11 Ibid., 15.
12 *Sermon on Mount,* II, 16.
13 Sermon 56, 5.
14 Sermon 213, 1.
15 *Sermon on Mount,* II, 16.
16 Sermon 57, 2.
17 Sermon 59, 2.
18 Sermon 58, 2.
19 *Sermon on Mount,* II, 19.
20 Sermon 56, 5.
21 Ibid.
22 Sermon 57, 4.
23 Sermon 58, 3.
24 Sermon 59, 3.
25 On Psalm 103 — 1st — 3.
26 Serm. Dom. II, 20.
27 Sermon 59, 4.
28 Sermon 56, 6.
29 Sermon 57, 5.
30 Sermon 58, 3.
31 Sermon 56, 7.
32 Ibid., 8.
33 *Sermon on Mount,* II, 17.
34 Sermon 57, 6.
35 *Sermon on Mount,* II, 23.
36 Sermon 57, 6-7.
37 *Sermon on Mount,* II, 27.
38 Sermon 56, 9.
39 Sermon 58, 5.
40 Sermon 56, 10.
41 Sermon 58, 5.
42 Sermon 57, 7.
43 Sermon 58, 5.
44 Serm. Dom. II, 26.
45 Sermon 59, 6.
46 On Psalm 103 — 1st — 19.
47 Serm. Dom. II, 28.
48 Ibid.
49 Ibid., II, 29.
50 Sermon 56, 11.
51 Sermon 56, 13.
52 Ibid., 14.
53 Ibid.
54 Ibid., 15.
55 Ibid., 16.
56 Ibid., 17.